THE POLLINATOR GARDEN

HOW TO ATTRACT NATURE'S HEROES - PLANTING FOR BIRDS, BEES, AND BUTTERFLIES

DIAN EATON

PAINTED SUNSET PUBLISHING LLC.

CONTENTS

For my daughter, Kim.

The journey continues.

INTRODUCTION

With a cup of steaming coffee in your hand, you step outside to enjoy the morning. You close your eyes, breathe deeply, and prepare for the energy of your sanctuary to fill your senses. Now imagine there is nothing. Imagine there are no sounds, no smells, no life to revive you. Imagine stepping into a garden and finding it eerily silent, with no buzzing of bees, no fluttering of butterflies, no cheerful visits of hummingbirds. Imagine a world without pollinators.

This isn't a doomsday prediction. This is a real possibility we face today. Pollinators are under threat, and their decline has devastating consequences for our food system, biodiversity, and ecosystems. But here's the good news: we can all play a part in turning this situation around, starting in our very own gardens. We, the gardeners, the guardians and caretakers of the land we oversee, can work together to prepare, protect, and provide for pollinators.

I am Dian Eaton, a home gardener and author. My first gardening book, *The Meadow Garden - Create a Low-Maintenance Wildflower and Native Plant Wonderland,* is a look into nature-forward gardening - using native plants - to develop a sustainable, organic, natural garden. While working on this book, I realized that creating a garden that brings joy and beauty could also serve a greater purpose. As gardeners, we try to do what is best for the land, working with nature, not against her, but perhaps we all could take gardening a step further.

My journey as a gardener began in beautiful Southern California, where I first fell in love with gardening. What started as a casual hobby bloomed into a love of nature, of getting my hands in the dirt and forgetting everything but what I was doing at that moment. That passion has grown over the years, whether I am working in a garden or on a tiny patio. I now see a bigger picture where gardeners everywhere can help support our struggling pollinator populations. And it won't be hard to do. All it takes is a little understanding, preparation, and optimism.

The Pollinator Garden: How to Attract Nature's Heroes - Planting for Birds, Bees, and Butterflies is more than just a follow-up to *The Meadow Garden*; it's a deep dive into the crucial role pollinators play in our world and the practical steps we can all take to support them. Through a mix of research, accessible advice, and personal anecdotes, I hope to guide gardeners of all levels in creating thriving pollinator gardens. This book isn't just about planting flowers; it's about understanding the ecological significance of pollinators, choosing the right plants for your region, and adding features that will turn your garden into a pollinator paradise.

In these pages, you'll find region-specific plant guides and garden plans for pollinator-friendly native plants in your area. You will learn all about pollinators: who they are, how they work, and what they need to continue their work. You will learn about planning and planting your garden, selecting the right plants, and more. This book is an invitation to begin a very personal journey. You will see yourself as an active participant in a larger story of ecological stewardship.

So, let's roll up our sleeves and get our hands dirty. Together, we can create spaces that dazzle the senses and support the unsung heroes of our ecosystems. We'll be doing our part. Even if no one sees the bigger picture, it won't matter—we'll know.

Welcome to *The Pollinator Garden*—a journey into the heart of nature's most vital players and a step toward a more sustainable and vibrant future.

1

THE ROLE OF POLLINATORS IN OUR ECOSYSTEM

" "The truth is: the natural world is changing. It is the most precious thing we have and we need to defend it."

— *DAVID ATTENBOROUGH*

One sunny spring day, you notice a butterfly fluttering around your garden. Its wings are bright and colorful, and while the butterfly is beautiful to watch, it's also doing something very important for the planet. It is performing a task that sustains the web of life itself: pollination. This butterfly, along with myriad other creatures, plays a pivotal role in the reproduction of plants, a process upon which our food supply precariously depends.

In this chapter, we'll learn how pollination works. We'll look at the different animals that help pollinate plants, how pollination happens, and how animals and plants work together in this process. Understanding this will help us see the bigger picture— how important these animals are not just for the beauty of nature but also for growing our food, supporting our ecosystem, and keeping our economy running.

Throughout this book, you will encounter the terms "**biodiversity**" and "**ecosystem.**" These terms are often confused, and people frequently ask if they are the same. They are not. Biodiversity refers to the variety of plant and animal species living and interacting within an environment. In contrast, an ecosystem is a geographic area where plants, animals, and other organisms coexist and interact within their environment. Various ecosystems exist, including deserts, oceans, lakes, plains, and forests. Biodiversity plays a crucial role in maintaining the stability of natural ecosystems and their capacity to produce oxygen, create soil, and purify water, benefiting both plant and animal communities and human society.

WHO ARE THE POLLINATORS?

The term "**pollinators**" refers to a vital group of animals that help our ecosystems by assisting in plant reproduction and have been doing so for millions of years. These tiny creatures are crucial for pollination. Over 1,200 types of crops and more than 180,000 plant species need pollination to survive. Without pollinators, life as we know it wouldn't exist.

Beyond the well-known bees, the pollinator group includes **butterflies, moths, birds, bats, beetles, ladybugs,** and even small mammals such as **lizards, rodents, honey possums, lemurs,** and **monkeys.** However, only about 9% of birds and mammals are pollinators.

Going forward with pollinator gardening, the pollinators we most want to attract to our gardens will be **birds, bees, butterflies,**

moths, bats, beetles, and **ladybugs.** Let's get to know these **Nature's Heroes.**

Bees

Most pollinators are insects, among which bees are considered vital for pollinating numerous crops. Globally, there are more than 20,000 species of bees, with about 3,600 native species found in North America and Canada.

Native Bees

Native bees usually nest by themselves, while the more social **BUMBLE BEES** (also native) create nest colonies underground. **HONEY BEE** colonies are concentrated in a single hive built in trees or similar places above ground. They may contain more than 50,000 bees. Both native bumble bees and honey bees gather pollen for food and produce honey in their nests or hives. Because flying expends a great deal of energy, bee nests are positioned close to food sources. However, if food resources are scarce, the bees can fly from a few hundred feet to a mile for food.

There are several physical differences that separate the appearance of the Bumble Bees from the Honey Bees: bumble bees are rounder and fuzzier than honey bees, which are more slender. Bumble bees, about 1 inch long, look almost like a single rounded section due to their plump shape, while honey bees have clearly separated body parts. Bumble bees are covered in thick hairs, making them excellent pollinators. In contrast, honey bees have fewer hairs. Both types of bees carry pollen in special 'baskets' on their hind legs, unique to these bees in North America.

Bumble bees are crucial for pollination and are larger than many other bee species in North America. Their big, hairy bodies generate a positive electric charge as they fly, which helps them attract negatively charged pollen. This feature, and their ability to cover more surface area, makes them highly effective at collecting pollen. Bumble bees can also perform "buzz pollination," essential for fertilizing plants like blueberries and tomatoes, where vibrations from their flight muscles release pollen. Bumble bees are adapted to cold climates and "shiver" to warm up and start foraging early in the spring, unlike honey bees that wait for warmer conditions.

The following are some of the native flowers frequented by native bees:

- **Asters** (symphyotrichum spp.)
- **Bee Balms, Bergamots** (monarda spp.)
- **Blazing Stars** (liatris spp.)
- **Giant Hyssops** (agastache spp.)
- **Goldenrods** (solidago spp.)
- **Lupines** (lupinus spp.)
- **Milkweeds** (asclepias spp.)
- **Native Onions and Garlics** (allium spp.)
- **Prairie Clovers** (dalea spp.)
- **Sunflowers** (helianthus spp.)
- **Wild Indigos** (baptisia spp.)

Honey Bees

The most recognized bee in North America is the **HONEY BEE**; although honey bees are not native to these regions, they were brought over by the colonists in 1622.

HONEY BEES are the only bees that make enough honey to share with humans. In addition, they also provide us with beeswax and propolis. Propolis is a sticky substance made from plants and sap. Honey bees use it to build and fix their hives. They seal gaps and smooth walls to protect against animals like snakes and lizards and to keep out bad weather like wind and rain. Propolis is also used medicinally in treatments for colds, upper respiratory infections, flu symptoms, healing wounds, burns, acne, cold sores, herpes, and neurodermatitis.

The flowers that attract honey bees often diminish in hot and dry weather when nectar stops flowing. These periods are known as summer nectar "dearths." However, dearths can occur at other times of the year as well. By growing plants that do well in many conditions, especially those that bloom in summer, you can help honey bees find food when it's hard to do so.

The following are some of the native flowers frequented by Honey Bees:

- **Anise Hyssop** (agastache foeniculum)
- **Asters** (symphyotrichum spp.)
- **Buckwheats** (eriogonum spp.)
- **Cornflowers** (echinacea spp.)
- **Fireweed** (chamerion angustifolium)
- **Goldenrods** (solidago spp.)
- **Ironweeds** (vernonia spp.)
- **Joe Pye** (eurochium spp.)
- **Milkweeds** (asclepias spp.)
- **Phacelia** (phacelia spp)
- **Sumacs** (rhus spp.)
- **Sunflowers** (helianthus spp.)

HONEY BEES are fascinating creatures that are integral not only to natural ecosystems but also to human agriculture. Here are five interesting facts about them:

1. **Incredible Navigators**: Honey bees are renowned for their navigation skills, utilizing the sun as a compass. Even on cloudy days, they can find their way, thanks to their ability to detect polarized light, which helps them infer the sun's location.
2. **Complex Communication**: They communicate through a series of dance moves known as the "waggle dance." By performing this dance, a bee can share detailed information with its hive mates about the direction and distance to sources of food (flowers), water, or new locations for the hive.
3. **Unique Role of the Queen Bee**: In a bee colony, the queen bee is the only female that can reproduce. She can lay up to

2,000 eggs per day during her peak season. The queen's sole purpose is to ensure the hive's survival by continuously laying eggs, and she is fed and cared for by worker bees.

4. **Environmental Impact**: Bees play a crucial role in pollinating plants. About one-third of the food that humans consume each day relies on pollination, mainly by bees. This includes fruits, vegetables, and nuts, highlighting the critical role bees play in our food supply and ecosystem health.

5. **Honey Production**: To produce a single pound of honey, a hive of bees must fly approximately 55,000 miles and visit 2 million flowers. Honey bees convert nectar into honey by a process of regurgitation and evaporation, storing it as a source of food for the colony, especially during winter.

Honey Bee Pollination

Bees are among the most effective and important pollinators, playing a crucial role in the growth of many types of plants, including those that produce fruit, vegetables, and nuts. Their pollination process is both fascinating and complex, involving several key steps and adaptations that make bees particularly efficient at transferring pollen between flowers. Here's how bees pollinate plants:

1. **Flower Attraction**: Bees are attracted to flowers by their colors, shapes, and scents. Flowers have evolved to display these signals that can effectively attract bees. Once a bee lands on a flower, it starts looking for nectar, a sweet liquid produced by plants as a reward for pollinators.

2. **Collecting Nectar and Pollen**: A bee collects nectar using its long, tube-shaped tongue called a proboscis, which

brushes against the flower's reproductive organs, picking up pollen on its body. Many bees also actively collect pollen, packing it into special structures on their legs called pollen baskets (corbiculae) to bring back to their hive for food.

3. **Cross-Pollination**: When the bee visits the next flower, some of the pollen from the first flower gets transferred to the stigma (the female reproductive part) of the second flower. This process, known as cross-pollination, is essential for the fertilization of many plants, leading to the production of seeds.

4. **Specialization and Efficiency**: Some bee species are specialized and will only visit the flowers of specific plant species, which can increase the efficiency of pollination. Even generalist species, like honeybees, exhibit behaviors such as flower constancy, where an individual bee prefers to visit only one type of flower during each foraging trip, enhancing the likelihood of successful pollination.

5. **Communication**: Bees are social insects, and many species, like honeybees, communicate with their hive mates about the location of food sources through a series of movements known as the "waggle dance." This behavior allows other bees in the colony to find the most productive flowers, ensuring efficient pollination.

Bumble Bees

BUMBLE BEES have distinct differences from Honey Bees, including how they make honey and how much honey they make. Bumble bees produce honey on a smaller scale, and it is intended for immediate use by the colony rather than long-term storage or human consumption. Here's what sets bumble bee honey production apart:

1. **Limited Quantities**: Bumble bees produce honey in much smaller quantities than honey bees, usually only enough to feed the colony for a few days. Their colonies usually consist of a few dozen to a couple of hundred bees, compared to honey bee hives, which can house tens of thousands of bees.
2. **Honey Storage**: Bumble bees store their honey in small pots made of wax, which are different from the hexagonal honeycomb cells used by honey bees. These pots are used to feed the colony, especially to sustain the queen and developing larvae.
3. **Feeding Habits**: The honey made by bumble bees serves as a vital food source during bad weather when workers

cannot go out to forage and feed the young. It provides the energy needed for the colony's survival and growth.

4. **Honey Characteristics**: The honey produced by bumble bees is similar to that of honey bees in its basic composition, but it is generally not harvested by humans due to the small amounts produced and because collecting it can harm or destroy the bumble bee colony.

5. **Colony Lifecycle**: Unlike honey bees, which can maintain their colonies through the winter, most bumble bee colonies are annual. The colony is started in the spring by a single queen and dies out by late autumn, with only new queens surviving the winter to start new colonies the following year. This lifecycle affects how and why bumble bees produce honey.

Bumble Bee Pollination

BUMBLE BEES are excellent pollinators. They play a crucial role in pollinating wildflowers as well as important agricultural crops. Their effectiveness as pollinators is due to several unique characteristics and behaviors:

1. **Generalist Foragers**: Bumble bees are not as selective as some other pollinators. They visit a wide variety of flowers, which helps ensure the pollination of many plant species.

2. **Buzz Pollination**: Bumble bees perform a special type of pollination known as buzz pollination or sonication. This involves vibrating their flight muscles while holding onto the flower, causing pollen to shake loose from the anther. This method is particularly effective for pollinating plants with flowers that keep their pollen inside, such as tomatoes, blueberries, and eggplants.

3. **Cold Tolerance**: Bumble bees have the ability to control their body heat by shivering and soaking up sunlight. This adaptation lets them stay active in cold weather and during the early spring and late fall, times when other pollinators might not be active.

4. **Strong Flight Capabilities**: Bumble bees' strong bodies and powerful flight muscles make them capable of working in tough weather conditions, like rain and cooler temperatures, that other pollinators can't handle. This trait makes them reliable pollinators over a longer part of the growing season.

5. **Local Movement and Colonies**: Bumble bees, unlike honey bees, form colonies that only last for a year and die out each winter, except for the mated queens, who survive the winter and begin new colonies in the spring. This cycle contributes to the pollination of many plants because the new queens frequently set up their nests far apart, covering large areas.

The connection between bees and plants is vital to our environment, playing a crucial role in nurturing plants and providing food for a variety of creatures, including us.

Birds

Hummingbirds

HUMMINGBIRDS are truly remarkable birds, known for their vibrant colors, their unmatched flying abilities, and their roles as pollinators in ecosystems across the Americas. Here are some interesting facts about the "Jewels of the Sky":

1. **Hovering Experts**: Hummingbirds are the only birds that can fly backward. They achieve this unique capability through the incredibly rapid flapping of their wings, which can beat up to 80 times per second in some species. This ability allows them to hover in place while accessing nectar from flowers and maneuver with precision in any direction.

2. **High Metabolism**: Hummingbirds have an extraordinarily high metabolism to support their rapid wing movement and energetic lifestyle. To fuel their energy needs, they consume roughly half their weight in sugar each day, visit

hundreds of flowers to drink nectar, and occasionally catch insects and spiders for protein.

3. **Long Migrations**: Some hummingbird species undertake remarkable migrations. For instance, the Ruby-throated Hummingbird migrates over 2,000 miles between Central America and North America, crossing the Gulf of Mexico in a non-stop flight that can take up to 20 hours.

4. **Rapid Heart Rate**: During flight, a hummingbird's heart can beat as fast as 1,260 beats per minute. Even at rest, their heart rate can exceed 200 beats per minute, which is necessary to support their intense flying activity and high metabolism.

5. **Vibrant Colors**: Hummingbirds display some of the most vibrant and diverse colors found in the bird world, but these colors don't come from pigments. Instead, the bright and often iridescent colors of a hummingbird's feathers come from the way the feathers are structured, reflecting and refracting sunlight to create the vivid colors we see.

Hummingbird Pollination

The pollination process of hummingbirds involves a unique interaction with flowers, tailored by mutual evolutionary adaptations. Here's how hummingbirds pollinate plants:

1. **Attraction to Bright Colors**: Hummingbirds are attracted to brightly colored flowers, especially red, pink, and orange hues. Unlike many insects, hummingbirds do not rely on floral scents, as they have a poor sense of smell. Instead, the vibrant colors of flowers serve as visual cues to guide them to nectar sources.

2. **Hovering and Feeding**: Unlike most birds, hummingbirds can hover in mid-air by rapidly flapping their wings,

which allows them to feed on nectar while in flight. This ability is crucial for accessing nectar from flowers that are designed to accommodate their feeding habits. As they hover, their heads come into contact with the flower's reproductive structures, the stamen (male part), and the pistil (female part).

3. **Transfer of Pollen**: While feeding on nectar, a hummingbird's head or throat often brushes against the flower's anthers, picking up pollen. When the bird visits the next flower, some of this pollen is transferred to the stigma, leading to pollination. This process is highly efficient, with hummingbirds visiting hundreds of flowers in a single day.

4. **Long Bills and Tongues**: Many hummingbirds have long, slender bills and extendable tongues. This shape fits well with the long parts of flowers that are meant for hummingbird pollination, making sure the bird can easily reach the flower's reproductive parts. Their long tongues can extend far beyond their beaks to reach nectar inside flowers, but when retracted, they coil up inside the bird's head. The structure of a hummingbird's head is designed to accommodate the long, extendable tongue without wrapping around the brain.

5. **Specialized Flowers**: Flowers that are adapted for hummingbird pollination have features that help with successful pollination. These include tube-shaped flowers that fit the bird's bill, strong parts that can support a hovering bird, and strategic placement of stamens and pistils to ensure contact with the bird. Additionally, these flowers often produce nectar throughout the day to attract hummingbirds.

The relationship between hummingbirds and the flowers they pollinate is a prime example of coevolution, where both the bird and the plant have developed traits that benefit each other. Through their pollination activities, hummingbirds not only sustain their nectar diet but also play a pivotal role in the reproduction of many plant species, contributing to the biodiversity of their ecosystems.

Other Bird Pollinators:

Many **OTHER BIRDS** around the world also contribute significantly to pollination, visiting flowers for their nectar and, in the process, transferring pollen between flowers. Here are a few examples of other important bird pollinators:

Sunbird

1. SUNBIRDS: Found primarily in Africa, Asia, and the Pacific Islands, sunbirds are colorful birds that play a similar role in their ecosystems to hummingbirds in the Americas. They have long, curved beaks and brush-tipped tongues designed for nectar feeding, and they are important pollinators for many tropical plants.

Flowerpecker

2. FLOWERPECKERS: In Asia, flowerpeckers and some species of sunbirds contribute to the pollination of a variety of plants through their nectar-feeding habits. They are especially important in pollinating plants in forest ecosystems.

3. HONEYEATERS: Native to Australia and New Guinea, honeyeaters are a diverse group of birds that feed on nectar, fruit, and insects. Their feeding behavior on nectar makes them important pollinators, especially of native Australian flora.

Honeyeater

4. BANANAQUITS: These small birds are found in Central and South America and the Caribbean. Bananaquits have a curved bill and feed on nectar from a variety of flowers, contributing to the pollination of many tropical plants.

Bananaquit

5. BELLBIRDS: Bellbirds are any of several unrelated birds from around the world that are named for their ringing voices. They have a brush-like tongue used to reach deeply into flowers to source nectar but also feed on fruits and insects. When feeding on nectar, they help pollinate many native trees and shrubs. By eating the fruits that grow after pollination, they also spread their seeds in their droppings, aiding in forest regeneration in two ways.

Bellbird

6. HONEYCREEPERS: In Hawaii, honeycreepers are a group of small birds related to finches and endemic to Hawaii. Both sexes sing in beautifully chiming choruses. Honeycreepers are small, and many have thin, down-curved bills; the tongue is brushy and may be double-tubed. In their roles as pollinators, many honeycreepers feed on nectar, and some are often called sugarbirds.

Honeycreeper

Other Bird Pollination

1. **Attracted to Bright Flowers**: Birds that pollinate are often attracted to bright, colorful flowers, especially those in shades of red, orange, and yellow. Unlike insects, birds can see red, and many bird-pollinated flowers have evolved to exploit this visual preference. The flowers tend to be large and sturdy enough to support the weight of their bird visitors.
2. **Nectar Feeding**: Like hummingbirds, other nectar-feeding birds have long beaks and tongues specially adapted for reaching into flowers. As they feed on nectar, their heads or beaks come into contact with the flower's reproductive organs, transferring pollen from one flower to another. This process is facilitated by the flower's design, which often positions the stamens and pistils to maximize contact with the bird.
3. **Specialized Flower Shapes**: Flowers pollinated by birds typically have shapes that are conducive to bird pollination. They may be tubular, providing a perfect fit for the bird's beak, or have a platform for the bird to perch on while feeding. This design ensures that the bird will come into close contact with the flower's pollen, facilitating effective pollination.
4. **High Energy Reward**: Bird-pollinated flowers usually produce a significant amount of nectar, which is a high-energy food source for birds. This abundant nectar reward encourages birds to visit multiple flowers, increasing the chances of cross-pollination.
5. **Diurnal Activity**: While many insects pollinate at night, bird pollination typically occurs during the day. This diurnal activity pattern means that bird-pollinated plants

can take advantage of daylight hours to attract their avian pollinators.

Plants and animals have evolved to support each other. Bird pollinators have formed beneficial relationships with certain plants where the birds receive nectar and, in return, assist in the plant's reproduction by transferring pollen. Flowers have adapted to attract birds with bright colors and strong shapes to hold their weight and nectar.

Butterflies

BUTTERFLIES are among the most beautiful and intriguing creatures in the animal kingdom, with a wide variety of species displaying an array of colors, patterns, and behaviors. Here are five interesting facts about butterflies:

1. **Sensory Antennae**: Butterflies use their antennae not only for balance but also for smell. Their antennae contain sensors that help them find food, locate mates, and navigate through their environment. This sense of smell is

so refined that they can detect nectar from flowers several meters away.

2. **Thermoregulation Tactics**: Butterflies cannot fly if their body temperature is too low. They are cold-blooded and rely on external heat sources to warm up. You'll often see butterflies basking in the sun with their wings spread wide open to absorb heat and warm their muscles enough to fly. Some species can also regulate their temperature by shivering.

3. **Vibrant Colors for Communication**: The colors and patterns on butterfly wings serve multiple purposes, from camouflage to warning predators of their toxicity. Bright colors can signal to mates and rivals alike. These colors are created either by the pigmentation of the wings or by the way their microscopic structures refract light.

4. **Incredible Journeys**: While the monarch butterfly is most famous for its long-distance migration, many butterfly species undertake significant journeys. These migrations can span hundreds to thousands of miles, often crossing countries and continents to escape seasonal changes.

5. **Life Span Variability**: The lifespan of butterflies varies greatly between species. While most adult butterflies live only a few weeks, some species, like the monarch, can live several months, especially those that migrate long distances. The entire lifecycle from egg to adult can span from about a month to a whole year, depending on the species and environmental conditions.

Monarch Butterflies

Monarch Butterflies

MONARCH BUTTERFLIES are among the most recognizable and studied butterflies in the world, celebrated for their beauty and incredible migratory patterns. Here are five interesting facts about monarch butterflies:

1. **Remarkable Migration**: Monarch butterflies undertake a remarkable migration every year, covering thousands of miles from North America to central Mexico to spend the winter. This journey is unique because it involves several generations of monarchs; the butterflies that return to Mexico are not the same ones that left but are their descendants, guided by innate instincts to the same wintering locations.

2. **Distinctive Appearance**: Monarchs stand out with their bright orange wings, marked by black lines and white spots. This striking appearance warns predators of their toxicity, a protective trait gained from eating milkweed plants as caterpillars. Milkweed contains toxic chemicals known as cardenolides, which make monarchs poisonous

to potential threats.

3. **Life Cycle Stages**: The life of a monarch butterfly goes through four steps: egg, caterpillar, chrysalis, and adult butterfly. This change, called metamorphosis, takes about a month. The monarch's change from a caterpillar on the ground to a flying butterfly is one of the most amazing examples of metamorphosis in nature.

4. **Role in Ecosystems**: Monarch butterflies are important for their ecosystems because they help flowers and plants reproduce by pollinating them. They also help milkweed plants, which they use for laying eggs, by spreading milkweed seeds around.

5. **Conservation Status**: Monarch butterfly numbers have been going down because of losing their homes, changes in the climate, and pesticide use. They are especially affected by the loss of milkweed plants they need to breed. Efforts to conserve their habitats and protect the species are underway, including planting milkweed and creating butterfly-friendly spaces in gardens.

Butterflies, with their preference for specific types of flowers and their method of feeding, play a crucial role in the cross-pollination of many plant species and the production of fruits and seeds.

Butterfly Pollination

Butterflies are important pollinators, playing a significant role in the pollination of various flowering plants. Their method of pollination involves several key behaviors and physical characteristics that facilitate the transfer of pollen between flowers. Here's how butterflies contribute to the process of pollination:

1. **Visual Attraction to Flowers**: Butterflies like bright and colorful flowers because they can see many colors, even

ultraviolet. The colors of flowers help show butterflies where to find nectar. They are especially drawn to red, purple, pink, and yellow flowers, more so than bees.

2. **Feeding on Nectar**: When a butterfly drinks nectar from a flower, it uses a long, curled-up part called a proboscis, like a straw, to reach the nectar inside deep flowers. This helps pollinate flowers that have deep corollas.

3. **Contact with Reproductive Parts of Flowers**: As a butterfly moves from flower to flower, parts of its body, usually the legs and underside, come into contact with the stamens (male reproductive organs) and collect pollen. When the butterfly visits another flower, some of this pollen rubs off on the stigma (female reproductive part), leading to pollination.

4. **Prefer Specific Flowers**: Butterflies prefer flowers that have flat tops or lots of room to land because it makes it easier for them to eat. Such flowers often have a design that makes it easy to transfer pollen between the butterfly and the flower.

5. **Daytime Pollinators**: Butterflies are daytime (diurnal) creatures, so they help pollinate flowers that are open and ready to be pollinated in the daytime. This daytime activity supports the work of other pollinators like moths and bats, which are active and pollinate at night.

Moths

Moth

MOTHS, often overshadowed by their butterfly cousins, are fascinating creatures with their own unique features and behaviors. While butterflies and moths help plants reproduce by pollinating them, their bigger yet less noticed role is as food for other animals. They are essential in the diet of various creatures, including birds, lizards, and even grizzly bears. For example, a grizzly bear can eat up to 30,000 moths daily during summer. Making up about 11% of all animal biodiversity, the role of butterflies and moths is crucial yet often overlooked. Here are some interesting facts about moths:

1. **Vast Diversity**: There are over 160,000 species of moths worldwide, compared to about 17,500 species of butterflies. Moths are incredibly diverse in size, color, and habitat, with new species still being discovered. Their variety makes them one of the most common and diverse types of animals in the world.
2. **Nighttime Pollinators**: While butterflies are known as

daytime pollinators, many moths play a crucial role in pollinating plants at night.

3. **Camouflage Experts**: Moths are masters of disguise. Many species have evolved wing patterns that mimic their surroundings, such as leaves, bark, or even bird droppings. This camouflage helps protect them from predators during their daytime resting hours.

4. **Silk Production**: Some moth species, like the **Silkworm Moth**, are famous for producing silk. Humans have cultivated silkworms for thousands of years to harvest silk for fabric. The larvae spin their cocoons from a single silk thread that can be up to 900 meters long.

5. **Ultrasonic Communication**: Moths have developed a variety of defenses against their main predators, bats. Some moths can hear the ultrasonic sounds bats make when they hunt and can dodge them. Other moths make their own ultrasonic sounds to either mix up the bats or let them know they are unpalatable.

Moth Pollination

Moths, particularly nocturnal species, play a significant but often underappreciated role in pollinating plants. Their nocturnal activities complement those of daytime pollinators, ensuring a continuous pollination process for many plant species. Here's how moths contribute to pollination:

1. **Nighttime Pollination**: Moths are primarily active at night, making them key pollinators for plant species that bloom or release their scent after dark. These plants often have white or pale-colored flowers, making them more visible at night, and produce a strong scent to attract their moth pollinators.

2. **Seeking Nectar**: Similar to other pollinators, moths feed on the nectar of flowers. As they move from flower to flower, pollen sticks to their bodies, particularly to their furry thorax and abdomen, facilitating the transfer of pollen to other flowers for cross-pollination.

3. **Long Proboscis for Deep Flowers**: Many moths have a long, straw-like mouthpart called a proboscis, which they use to reach nectar located deep within flowers. The **Hawk Moth**, for example, has one of the longest proboscises of any pollinating insect, enabling it to pollinate deep flowers like the **moonflower** and certain **orchids**.

4. **Attraction to Specific Flowers**: Moth-pollinated flowers often exhibit specific traits that make them attractive to moths, such as being open at night, emitting a strong fragrance, and producing ample nectar. These traits ensure that moths can easily find and pollinate the flowers in the dark.

5. **Vital Role in Ecosystems**: Moths help plants mix genes and stay healthy by spreading pollen between flowers. They are especially helpful in places like tropical forests and deserts, where they help pollinate a wide variety of plant species.

By pollinating plants at night, moths ensure that pollination can occur around the clock, supporting the survival and reproduction of many plant species.

Beetles

Beetle

BEETLES are among the oldest pollinators, having contributed to the pollination of flowering plants for over 100 million years. Beetles represent the largest group of animal species on Earth and are the earliest known pollinators! About 400,000 beetle species have been identified so far. Their diversity and adaptability make them fascinating subjects of study. Here are some interesting facts about beetles:

1. **Enormous Diversity**: Beetles are the biggest group of animals on Earth, accounting for around 40% of all insect species identified. They inhabit almost every type of environment except for oceans and the polar ice regions. Their sizes vary greatly, from the very small **Featherwing Beetle** at just 0.02 inches to the large **Hercules Beetle**, which can grow to more than 6 inches long, including its horns.

2. **Unique Elytra**: Beetles have a special feature called elytra, which is the hard front wings. Unlike the wings of other

insects, elytra don't help beetles fly. Instead, they protect the beetle's fragile back wings and cover the top part of their bodies like a shield.

3. **Critical Ecological Roles**: Beetles play vital roles in their ecosystems, including pollination, breaking down dead plants and animals, and controlling the populations of other insects. **Dung beetles** are especially helpful because they recycle waste, make the soil better, and help spread seeds.

4. **Incredible Survivors**: Beetles have existed for an incredibly long time, with fossils showing they've been around for about 300 million years. Their success and survival over such a long period are largely due to their ability to adapt to many different environments.

5. **Bioluminescence**: Some beetles, like the well-known **Fireflies**, have the ability to produce light. This light, called bioluminescence, helps them find a mate, scare away enemies, or attract food. The light comes from a special chemical reaction inside parts of their abdomen.

Beetle Pollination

Beetles pollinate in a special way called "mess and soil," which is less tidy than how bees or butterflies do it. This method involves a few important actions and traits:

1. **Attraction to Flowers**: Unlike bees and butterflies that seek nectar, beetles usually go after pollen or floral tissues, which they consume. Many beetles are attracted to brightly colored flowers, but most prefer those that are white or dull-colored. These flowers often emit strong, fruity, or fermented smells that draw beetles in.

2. **Eating and Moving Pollen**: Beetles are accidental pollinators. While eating parts of flowers like pollen and petals, they move clumsily and get pollen stuck all over their bodies. Then, when they visit another flower to eat, they leave some of that pollen behind on the new flower, helping it to pollinate.

3. **Preference for Certain Flowers**: Flowers that beetles pollinate are designed to attract them. These flowers are usually big, shaped like bowls, and have lots of pollen that can handle the rough way beetles eat. Some plants depend on beetles to help them grow and spread because of this special way of pollination.

4. **Floral Morphology Adaptations**: Plants that beetles pollinate are strong enough to handle beetle bites and are designed so beetles easily brush against the pollen while feeding or moving around, helping the plant to be pollinated.

5. **Nighttime Activity**: Some beetles are active at night and like flowers that open or smell strong after dark. This night-time pollination is very important for some plants that need beetles and other insects that come out at night to help them pollinate.

While beetles are not as efficient at pollination as bees because of their less targeted approach, they are essential pollinators for a wide variety of plants, especially ancient species like **magnolias** and **water lilies**. Their role highlights the diversity of pollination strategies in the natural world and the complex interdependencies between insects and plants.

Bats

BATS are fascinating creatures, often misunderstood and surrounded by myths. They are vital to ecosystems around the globe for their roles as pollinators, seed dispersers, and insect controllers. Here are five interesting facts about bats:

Fruit Bat

1. **Only Flying Mammals**: Bats are the only mammals capable of sustained flight. Their wings are actually highly modified hands with skin stretched between their fingers, a structure like the wings of birds or insects. This unique anatomy allows them great agility and precision in the air.

2. **Echolocation Expertise**: Many bat species navigate and hunt their prey through echolocation. They emit high-frequency sounds that bounce off objects and return as echoes, enabling bats to create a sonic map of their surroundings, detect obstacles, and pinpoint insects even in complete darkness.

3. **Diverse Diets**: While the majority of bat species consume insects, their diets can be varied. Some species specialize in eating fruits, nectar, and pollen, playing crucial roles in pollinating plants and dispersing seeds. A few bats, like the infamous **Vampire Bats,** feed on the blood of other animals.

4. **Vital Environmental Roles**: Bats contribute greatly to the environment. Bats that eat insects keep pest numbers

down, reducing the need for chemical pesticides in agriculture. Fruit bats are key pollinators for many plants, including bananas, mangoes, and agave (used to make tequila), and spread seeds, which is especially important in tropical forests.

5. **Longevity and Reproduction**: Bats have unusually long lifespans for their size, with some species living more than 30 years. They typically have a slow reproduction rate, with most species giving birth to only one offspring per year. This low birth rate makes bat populations particularly vulnerable to threats such as habitat loss, disease, and climate change.

Bat Pollination

Bats are crucial pollinators in many ecosystems, particularly in tropical and desert environments. Their pollination work often occurs at night and involves a fascinating interplay between the bats and the plants they pollinate. Here's how bats contribute to pollination:

1. **Nighttime Activity**: Unlike many pollinators that are active during the day, bats work at night. This nocturnal behavior is perfectly suited for pollinating plants that open their flowers after dark. These plants typically produce strong scents to attract their bat pollinators.
2. **Seeking Nectar**: Plants that rely on bats for pollination have adapted in special ways to suit bats, like having large, sturdy flowers that can hold a bat's weight and have white or light colors that stand out in the dark. As bats feed on the flower's nectar, their faces or bodies come into contact with the flower's reproductive organs, transferring pollen in the process.

3. **Long-distance Travelers**: Bats can fly long distances every night, which makes them great at pollinating plants that are spread out or need cross-pollination over long ranges.

4. **Special Adaptations**: Some bats have special features like long tongues that let them reach deep into flowers to reach the nectar. These traits match well with the flowers they help pollinate, showing that bats and these plants have evolved together closely.

5. **Crucial for Certain Plants**: Bats are especially important for the pollination of certain types of plants, including many species of **agave**, bananas, mangoes, and guavas. In desert environments, they are vital for the pollination of cacti, including the iconic **Saguaro** and **Organ Pipe cacti.**

Bats helping with pollination highlights the different ways plants can be pollinated. It shows the importance of protecting bats to keep nature and farming healthy.

Lady Bugs

Ladybugs, also known as **ladybirds** or **lady beetles**, are beloved insects known for their distinctive spots and colors. Beyond their charming appearance, ladybugs play a significant role in agriculture and ecosystems by controlling pest populations. Here are some interesting facts about ladybugs:

1. **Diverse Species**: There are about 5,000 different species of ladybugs worldwide, varying in color, size, and number of spots. While the classic image of a ladybug is red with black spots, they can also be found in shades of yellow, orange, black, grey, and even pink, with some species having no spots at all.

2. **Aphid Hunters**: Ladybugs are voracious predators of aphids and other pest insects, making them beneficial allies in gardens and agricultural fields. A single ladybug can consume up to 5,000 aphids in its lifetime, helping to protect crops and plants from these harmful pests.

Ladybug

3. **Chemical Defense**: When threatened, ladybugs can release a yellow fluid from their legs, a process known as "reflex bleeding." This fluid contains toxic chemicals that deter predators, and its strong smell and taste make ladybugs unappetizing to would-be attackers.

4. **Winter Hibernation**: In cooler climates, ladybugs hibernate through the winter in large groups under leaf litter, rocks, or other sheltered spots. They often cluster together to stay warm, sometimes in the thousands, and their combined body heat helps them survive the cold.

5. **Symbolism and Names**: Ladybugs are considered symbols of good luck in many cultures. The name "ladybug" originated in Europe during the Middle Ages when the insects were dedicated to the Virgin Mary and called "Our Lady's beetle." The spots on their backs were said to symbolize the Seven Sorrows of Mary.

Ladybug Pollination

Ladybugs are not considered major pollinators like bees or butterflies. However, they contribute to the pollination process in an incidental manner. Here's how:

1. **Accidental Pollinators**: As ladybugs move across flowers in search of aphids and other prey, they may accidentally come into contact with the pollen of a flower. When they move to another flower to continue their hunt, they can unknowingly transfer some of this pollen, helping to fertilize the plant.

2. **Nectar and Pollen as Food Sources**: Although their primary diet consists of other insects, ladybugs may also consume nectar and pollen, especially during times when their preferred food sources are scarce. In doing so, they unintentionally pick up and transfer pollen as they move from flower to flower.

3. **Generalist Foragers**: Ladybugs do not specialize in visiting specific types of flowers, so their potential as pollinators is spread across various plant species. This generalist behavior increases their chances of unintentionally contributing to the pollination of a wide range of plants.

4. **Beneficial Presence in Ecosystems**: The presence of ladybugs in an ecosystem signifies healthy biological control of pest populations, which can indirectly support the health and reproductive success of flowering plants. By controlling pests that may damage flowers or spread diseases, ladybugs help maintain the overall balance of garden and agricultural ecosystems.

5. **Indicator of Biodiversity**: An abundance of ladybugs can indicate high biodiversity and a well-functioning ecosystem, where various types of pollinators, including those more efficient than ladybugs, can thrive. This diversity is crucial for robust plant pollination networks.

The seven pollinators showcased above are the primary pollinators. Their role in pollination is critical for the reproduction of the majority of flowering plants.

2

UNDERSTANDING POLLINATION

"*If you wish to make anything grow, you must understand it, and understand it in a very real sense. 'Green fingers' are a fact, and a mystery only to the unpracticed. But green fingers are the extensions of a verdant heart.*"

— *RUSSELL PAGE, THE EDUCATION OF A GARDENER*

HOW IT WORKS AND WHY IT MATTERS

Pollination Process: Pollination is the process of moving pollen from one flower part to another to fertilize plants, often happening when insects and animals searching for nectar carry pollen between flowers. While some plants use wind or water for pollination, many rely on animals. This process is crucial for plants to produce seeds and new plants.

Diversity of Pollinators: The diversity among pollinators is staggering. This is not just a marvel of nature but shows just how many ways nature has devised to do the job of pollination, making sure plants can grow and spread in many different environments.

Insects have evolved their own methods of packing in the pollen and nectar, which, for many insects, has to do with their fuzzy appearance. Pollen is not loose like dust but is electrostatically sticky and sticks to the oppositely charged fuzzy hairs on the insect's body. This allows the pollen to transfer when the insect moves on. Conversely, when the insect lands on another flower, the pollen is rubbed onto that flower, completing the transfer.

Interdependence: The relationship between pollinators and plants is very close and has developed over millions of years. Flowers have evolved, changing their shapes, colors, and smells to attract certain pollinators, which in turn have changed to better reach the food plants provide. Some flowers are designed to be reached by only one type of pollinator. Both pollinators and plants depend on each other for survival, evolving together in unique ways.

Ecosystem Services: The role of pollinators extends far beyond the flowers they visit. They are crucial for keeping ecosystems healthy supporting the growth of fruits, seeds, and nuts that serve as food for a wide range of animals. In agriculture, pollinators help us grow many different crops, like fruits, vegetables, coffee, and chocolate, making them a key part of ensuring there's enough food for everyone around the world.

The economic value of pollination services highlights the indispensable role pollinators play in our food supply. More than 100 U.S. grown crops rely on pollinators. The added revenue to crop production from pollinators is valued at $18 billion. Honey bees are America's primary commercial pollinator, although there are over 4,000 types of bees in the United States. Today, there are about 2.8 million U.S. honey bee hives.

Pollination is a vital process happening in every flourishing garden. It's not just about adding beauty to our environment with bright colors and sweet scents; pollination is crucial for the survival of plant species and for keeping our food supply going. Let's take a closer look at how pollination works, the different ways it can happen, its key role in increasing the variety of life, and how it significantly impacts farming.

Mechanics of Pollination

Pollination of Flowering Plants

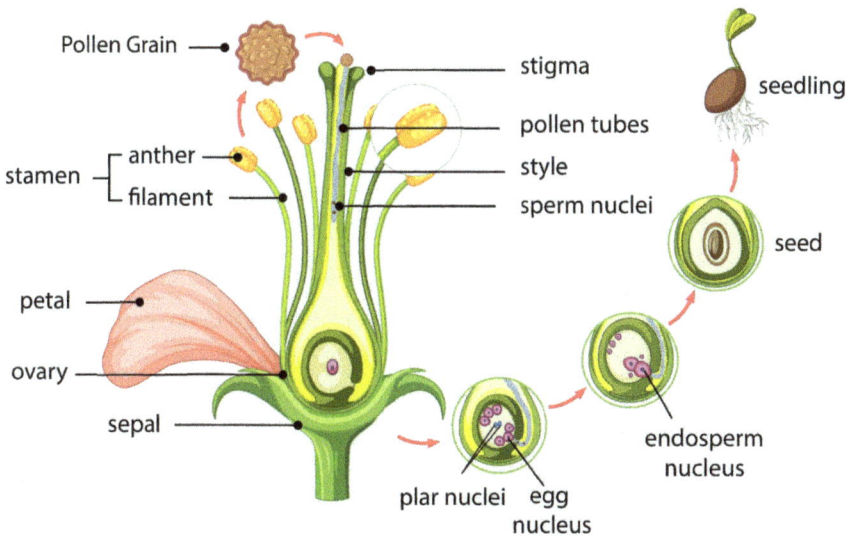

Pollination occurs when pollen grains from a flower's male part land on its female part, the stigma. This can be done by wind, water, or animals like bees, butterflies, and birds seeking nectar. As these pollinators feed, pollen attaches to them and is transferred to the next flower they visit, enabling fertilization. This process results in seeds and fruits, allowing plants to reproduce and sustain their species.

Variety of Pollination Methods

Pollination can happen in different ways, depending on what a plant needs. Self-pollination is when a flower fertilizes itself, which makes sure seeds are made but doesn't mix up the plant's genes much. Cross-pollination, where pollen moves between flowers of different plants, creates more gene variety and healthier plants. Some plants have special pollination methods just for certain pollinators like bees, birds, and bats. Each type of pollination helps make sure we have lots of different plants and healthy environments.

Importance for Biodiversity

Pollination is crucial for producing diverse plants, essential for a robust environment. By transferring pollen, pollinators like bees and butterflies help mix plant genes, enhancing plants' ability to adapt to environmental changes, resist pests, and maintain ecosystem stability. Additionally, the fruits and seeds from pollination feed many animals, creating an interconnected web of life that supports a broad range of species.

Impact on Agriculture

Pollination is crucial for agriculture and affects about one-third of our food, including fruits, vegetables, and crops for feeding animals like alfalfa and clover. Bees and butterflies are key pollinators and add billions of dollars to farming. They're vital not just for growing food but also for the overall supply of food worldwide.

Next, we take a look at the challenges pollinators face and how we can help. By doing so, we ensure that they keep playing an important role for future generations.

DECLINING POLLINATOR POPULATIONS: UNDERSTANDING THE THREATS

Pollinators are in trouble, which is unraveling ecosystems all over the world. Their numbers are dropping for many reasons, all making the situation worse. Understanding these threats is the first step toward solving the problem, ensuring the survival of these crucial species, and keeping our planet healthy.

Causes of Decline

Several major factors contribute to the decline of pollinator populations globally:

- **Habitat Loss**: Expanding urban development and aggressive agricultural practices have greatly reduced the natural habitats of pollinators. The natural spaces where pollinators live, like wildflower fields and forests, are disappearing. They're being replaced by monoculture crops and concrete jungles, leaving fewer places for pollinators to nest and feed.
- **Pesticide Use**: Using lots of chemical pesticides in farming and gardening can backfire. Although these chemicals are meant to keep pests away from crops, they often end up harming other creatures as well, including many pollinators.
- **Climate Change**: Changes in climate are causing plants to bloom at different times than pollinators are used to being

active. This mismatch results in pollinators having less
food and plants getting pollinated less often.

- **Disease**: Diseases, parasites, and harmful organisms, often
  spread by humans, are big dangers to pollinators. Varroa
  mites, for instance, are considered one of the most serious
  threats to honeybee populations worldwide. These mites
  attach themselves to the bodies of honeybees and feed on
  their bodily fluids. This weakens and damages the bees and
  can spread viruses and diseases within bee colonies,
  eventually causing the colony to collapse.

Consequences of Decline

The drop in pollinator numbers affects much more than just losing
different kinds of species. It impacts all parts of nature's network,
including:

- **Global Food Supply**: Many of our food crops rely on
  pollinators. Without them, we could face less stable food
  production, which might lead to food shortages and higher
  prices.
- **Variety of Plant Life**: Pollinators help many plant species
  reproduce. Their decline could lead to the loss of many
  plant species. This would harm ecosystems and the
  animals that depend on those plants for food and a place to
  live.
- **Ecosystem Services**: Pollinators do more than just
  pollinate. They also help control pests and recycle
  nutrients. If their numbers keep falling, these natural
  processes could be disrupted, hurting ecosystems around
  the world.

Examples of Pollinator Decline

Rusty-Patched Bumblebee

The Rusty-Patched Bumblebee: Once abundant across North America, the rusty-patched bumblebee has seen an 87% decline in its population over the last 20 years. Conservationists are trying to help by restoring its natural habitat and using fewer pesticides in critical areas.

The Monarch Butterfly: Known for its remarkable ability to fly long distances, the monarch butterfly's population has taken a dramatic decline, largely due to habitat loss and the reduction of milkweed plants essential for their breeding. Conservation efforts include

Monarch Butterfly

planting milkweed and keeping their winter homes safe.

Global and Local Perspectives

The decrease in pollinator populations is a global issue, but the effects and solutions can vary by location. For example, in Europe, the disappearance of wildflower habitats due to increased farming has led to Europe-wide efforts to bring back these natural spaces and use farming methods that are better for pollinators. At the same time, in local areas, gardeners and city officials are making special paths and safe spots for pollinators, offering them crucial refuges in urban settings.

The connection between efforts around the world and in our local areas shows that even though the problem is huge, the things we do as individuals and in our communities matter a lot. Knowing the needs and dangers pollinators face right where we live, we can take the actions needed to help them.

THE IMPACT ON OUR FOOD SUPPLY AND BIODIVERSITY

Pollinators are rightly called the unsung heroes of our food system, working behind the scenes to ensure the production of many of the crops we depend on daily. From fruits, vegetables, and nuts that provide essential proteins, pollinators play a pivotal role in bringing these food sources from the field to our tables. But when their numbers decline, it's not just a problem for farming; it's a problem affecting the variety of life on Earth and the health of our planet.

Pollinators and Food Crops

The teamwork of bees and other pollinators working with plants is the key to growing food worldwide. Imagine large almond farms; without bees, there'd be no almonds. It's the same with blueberries, cherries, and apples – they all need bees to help them make fruit. Sometimes, farmers even bring in bees just to ensure their crops get pollinated. Our food supply is closely linked to the well-being of bees and other pollinators.

Economic Implications

The economic stakes of bee-plant teamwork are high. Pollination helps the world's economy by billions because it plays such a critical role in agriculture. This isn't just about growing crops; it affects all parts of the food industry, including creating jobs and selling food. Losing pollinator services threatens to disrupt the entire economic engine, leading to increased costs for farmers, higher food prices for everyone, and less variety and fewer crops grown.

Biodiversity Loss

The problem of losing pollinators is big and affects more than just farming. Pollinators are crucial for wild plants to grow and stay healthy, contributing to genetic diversity and ecosystem resilience. The loss of pollinators will result in fewer plant species and will affect the animals that depend on those plants for food and habitat. If biodiversity keeps dropping, lively natural areas could turn into deserts, making it harder for nature to clean the air and water, keep the soil good for growing things, and control the climate.

Nutritional Consequences

The potential impact on human nutrition is equally concerning. Many foods that bees and other pollinators help grow are full of important nutrients like vitamins and antioxidants that we need to stay healthy. A decline in the availability of these food sources could lead to nutritional deficiencies, particularly in communities that heavily rely on pollinator-dependent crops. This diversity in our diet puts our overall food quality and supply at risk.

Pollinators are a crucial part of nature and our very survival. Their decline could impact our food supply, economic stability, the variety of life on Earth, and our health. The steps we take to protect these vital creatures will shape the future of our planet and our place within it.

THE IMPORTANCE OF POLLINATORS IN URBAN ENVIRONMENTS

In busy cities, among concrete and steel, bees and butterflies are finding unexpected homes. Though cities seem far from natural, they're becoming refuges for these pollinators.

Urban Pollinators

The idea of city pollinators shows how amazing these animals are at adapting. Bees, butterflies, and birds have learned to live in cities, using plants in yards, parks, and rooftop gardens. They move across the city, looking for nectar and pollen in these green spots. But it's not easy for them. They face problems like not having enough green areas and dealing with higher city temperatures, which can be tough on both the pollinators and the plants they need.

Benefits of Urban Pollinators

The presence of pollinators in urban areas brings a multitude of benefits:

- **Increased biodiversity**: City pollinators help make city plants more varied by pollinating flowers in gardens, parks, and natural areas.
- **Food security**: Urban gardens and community farms rely on pollinators to produce fruits, vegetables, and seeds.
- **Enhancement of urban green spaces**: Pollinators play a key role in the health and beauty of urban green spaces, supporting the growth of flowering plants, adding color and vitality to city landscapes, and making urban areas more livable and inviting for residents and visitors alike.

Designing Pollinator-Friendly Cities

Transforming cities into pollinator-friendly environments requires thoughtful design and planning. Several strategies have proven effective in supporting urban pollinator populations:

- **Pollinator pathways**: Pollinator pathways are like green bridges across cities, connecting places like parks, gardens, and natural areas so that pollinators can easily find food and places to live.
- **Use of native plants in landscaping**: Using local plants in city garden projects is crucial for helping the area's pollinators. These plants are used to the local climate and soil and have the exact type of nectar and pollen that native pollinators need.
- **Rooftop and balcony gardens**: In densely populated urban areas, rooftops and balconies offer valuable opportunities to create pollinator-friendly habitats.

Community Involvement

The push for cities friendly to pollinators comes from people, community groups, and local governments working together. It often begins with gardeners, nature lovers, and active community members. Here's how you can help:

- **Community gardens**: Getting involved in a community garden helps city pollinators by creating spaces full of different plants and flowers they need. These gardens also give people a chance to garden for fun, reduce stress, and connect with others in their area. It's good for everyone: the community, the pollinators, and the gardeners.
- **Educational programs**: Joining or setting up learning events can help more people understand why pollinators are important and inspire them to help. Schools, community centers, and local nature groups are perfect places for these activities.
- **Advocacy**: Engaging with local officials and participating in public meetings are effective ways to influence urban planning and environmental policies.

The revitalization of urban environments as havens for pollinators is an inspiring example of how cities can evolve to support both human and ecological health.

NATIVE POLLINATORS VS. HONEY BEES: WHO DOES WHAT?

Pollination isn't just about honey bees; it involves a wide range of helpers, especially native pollinators that have evolved alongside local plants for thousands of years. These native pollinators play a crucial role in maintaining healthy ecosystems. While honey bees are often highlighted for their pollination work, the equally important contributions of native pollinators are vital for our planet's well-being.

Role of Native Pollinators

Native pollinators like different kinds of bees, butterflies, moths, birds, and bats are crucial to their environments. Unlike honey bees, which can visit many types of plants, many native pollinators have evolved to work with specific plants. This special relationship helps both the pollinator and the plant survive. For example, the blueberry bee is perfect for pollinating blueberries because it shakes pollen loose at just the right speed. Also, some orchids depend entirely on one type of moth to pollinate them.

Comparison with Honey Bees

While honey bees are incredible pollinators, known for their role in commercial agriculture, they are not native to many parts of the world where they are now found. In these areas, native pollinators often surpass honey bees in pollination efficiency. For example, native squash bees are early risers, pollinating flowers like pumpkins and squashes before honey bees even begin their day. Furthermore, the reliance on a single species for pollination, such as the honey bee, can make our food system risky, promoting the need for multiple species of pollinators.

Challenges Facing Native Pollinators

Native pollinators face numerous threats that jeopardize their survival and the ecosystems they support. Bumble bees, for example, are having a hard time with climate change. Warmer weather forces them to move to higher elevations in search of habitats, only to find themselves with nowhere else to go. The growth of cities and farming breaks up their living spaces, leaving them with less food and fewer places to live. On top of that, pesticides and climate change make it harder for them by changing the timing of flowering or available habitats.

Supporting Native Pollinators

Fostering environments where native pollinators can thrive is not just beneficial for the natural world but essential for our survival. Here are practical steps to support these vital creatures:

- **Plant Native**: Pick plants from your area for your garden. These plants are used to your local weather and soil, so they need less water and care than non-native plants.
- **Create Habitat**: Besides planting, think about letting part of your yard stay wild or adding things like piles of branches or bare dirt spots to serve as nesting sites for ground-nesting bees and other pollinators.
- **Reduce Pesticide Use**: If you need to use pesticides, choose ones that only target specific pests and use them when pollinators are not around, like in the evening. Also, consider using only organic pest control methods that are less risky to pollinators.
- **Provide Water**: There are many water sources to consider, such as birdbaths with stones for landing spots.
- **Spread the Word**: Teach your neighbors, schools, and community about why native pollinators are important. Make your garden an example.

Helping pollinators is key to keeping nature healthy. Each type of pollinator plays a unique role in the circle of life. By learning about these creatures and helping them, we're not just looking after our environment but also making sure we have the resources we rely on.

CREATING HABITATS TO SUPPORT DIVERSE POLLINATOR SPECIES

Making your garden a home for pollinators is about more than just putting in flowers. A good habitat for them also has places to nest, water to drink, and is safe from harmful pesticides. This section will guide you through the steps needed to create a pollinator sanctuary, starting with the basics of what pollinators need.

Habitat Essentials

A successful pollinator habitat contains several critical elements:

- **Food Sources**: Pollinators need a steady supply of nectar and pollen as plants grow. It's important to have different kinds of flowers that bloom at various times.
- **Nesting Sites**: Bees and butterflies need special places to nest and lay eggs. Having different natural materials and quiet spots can help meet their needs.
- **Protection from Pesticides**: Minimizing or eliminating pesticide use is crucial to protect pollinators from harm. If pest control is necessary, opting for organic methods and targeting applications to avoid contact with beneficial insects is preferable.

Designing a Pollinator-Friendly Garden

Crafting a garden that meets the needs of a variety of pollinator species involves thoughtful planning. Here's how to approach it:

- **Assess Your Space**: First, look at the space, sunlight, and soil in your garden. This will show you which plants will do well and if you need to make any changes.
- **Incorporate Diversity**: Choose a mix of plants to bring many kinds of pollinators. Research the pollinators you specifically want to attract, and incorporate plants that will appeal to them. Have plants that are tall and short, different colors, and bloom at different times.
- **Create Structure**: Arrange your garden by putting plants in groups. This looks nice and helps pollinators find and move among the plants more easily.
- **Consider Water Sources**: Putting in a shallow water spot or a birdbath with rocks for landing gives pollinators the water they need.

Plant Selection

Choosing the right plants is perhaps the most critical step in creating a pollinator-friendly garden. Here are some tips for making those choices:

- **Opt for Native Plants**: Native plants are best suited for local pollinators and are usually more resilient and require less maintenance.
- **Ensure Continuous Bloom**: Select plants that bloom at different times to ensure a continuous supply of nectar and pollen from early spring to late fall.
- **Avoid Hybrid Plants**: Some hybrid plants might not have seeds or food for pollinators. Stick to heirloom and native varieties.
- **Plant in Clusters**: Planting in clusters rather than single plants can help attract more pollinators and enable them to feed more efficiently.

Maintenance Practices

Maintaining a pollinator-friendly garden goes beyond regular gardening practices. Here are some sustainable approaches to consider:

- **Organic Pest Control**: When dealing with pests, opt for organic solutions. Introducing beneficial insects, using neem oil, or employing physical barriers is another way to protect your garden without harming pollinators.
- **Mulching**: Applying a natural mulch helps retain soil moisture and suppress weeds but also provides a habitat for ground-nesting insects. Just be sure to leave some areas bare for those species that prefer it.
- **Avoiding Chemicals**: Create good soil by composting, which helps plants grow well on their own.
- **Regular Monitoring**: Watch your plants and pollinators closely. Noticing which plants attract specific pollinators can help you decide what to plant next and how to change your garden.

Adding these ideas to your garden care can make a great home for many types of pollinators. It doesn't matter if you have a big yard or just a small balcony garden; you can do things to help pollinators. Every flower you plant, every time you don't use pesticides, and every bit of water you offer helps these important animals that do so much for our planet.

THE BASICS OF POLLINATOR BIOLOGY AND BEHAVIOR

Pollinators have interesting behaviors and traits that are perfectly suited to their job in nature. By learning about when they're active and how they communicate, we can do a better job of helping them.

Understanding Pollinator Behavior

Pollinators have different ways of finding food that matches their natural patterns and where they live. Bees look for flowers during the day using their vision. Moths and bats work at night, using their strong sense of smell or sound waves to find flowers. This way, they don't compete much with each other, making pollination work better.

Pollinators like different flowers, often based on the flower's shape, color, and smell and how easy it is to get nectar and pollen. For example, hummingbirds prefer bright red flowers that fit their long beaks, making it easier for them to feed on nectar.

Life Cycles

Pollinators go through many stages in their lives, each with its own challenges. Knowing about these stages can help us make and care for our gardens in ways that support pollinators at every point in their lives.

- **Bees**: The life of a bee goes from egg to grown-up through different stages: egg, larva, pupa, and adult. Each stage needs certain things, like safety from predators and bad weather. Gardeners can help by putting up nesting boxes or leaving dead wood and untouched soil, giving bees safe places to lay eggs and grow.
- **Butterflies**: Butterflies change completely as they grow, from eggs on certain plants to caterpillars, then to pupae, and lastly, to grown-ups. The caterpillar stage needs lots of

food plants. Planting local milkweed and plants that caterpillars like to eat is really helpful for them.

- **Bats**: Bats are important pollinators in some places and have a simple life cycle but need safe roosting sites to rest. Putting up bat boxes can help them, especially in areas where natural roosts are scarce.

Pollinator Communication

Communicating with each other and to plants is an important part of how pollinators live. They use a variety of signals to do this:

- **Chemical signals**: Some plants give off special smells to draw in their pollinators. Like, some orchids can smell like the scent female bees make to attract male bees for pollination.
- **Visual cues**: Colors and designs are really important for getting pollinators to come to flowers. Bees, for example, are attracted to flowers that have patterns only they can see with ultraviolet light. These patterns help guide the bees directly to where the nectar is, like a runway for airplanes.
- **Acoustic signals**: Some pollinators talk with sounds. Male bees can buzz in a special way to get female bees' attention or to shake pollen out of flowers, which is called buzz pollination.

Adaptations for Pollination

Pollinators have changed over time to have special traits and behaviors that make them better at pollinating:

- **Specialized mouthparts**: Many pollinators have mouth parts shaped to fit how they eat. Hummingbirds have long, thin beaks to get nectar from deep flowers, and butterflies and moths have long, straw-like tongues to drink nectar.
- **Body hair**: Bees have small hairs all over them that catch pollen, making them highly effective at pollination. When they visit different flowers, these hairs rub against parts of the flower, helping move pollen around.
- **Wing shape and size**: Pollinators have wings that fit how they live. For example, hummingbirds can flap their wings very fast to stay in one spot in front of flowers, and butterflies have bigger wings that let them float smoothly from one flower to another.

Pollinators are deeply woven into nature. Their unique behaviors and features, from their activity times to their communication methods, highlight their intricate relationship with plants. As gardeners, understanding these qualities helps us build gardens that meet pollinators' needs and appreciate their role in nature. By choosing actions like planting diverse native plants, cutting down on pesticides, and creating homes for them, we can support pollinators' survival.

3

LAYING THE FOUNDATION FOR A FLOURISHING POLLINATOR SANCTUARY

> *"A garden requires patient labor and attention. Plants do not grow merely to satisfy ambitions or to fulfill good intentions. They thrive because someone expended effort on them."*

> — *LIBERTY HYDE BAILEY*

ASSESSING YOUR GARDEN SPACE

Imagine a garden where each plant, bit of sunlight, and spot of soil helps make a perfect place for pollinators. This can really happen, and it begins with knowing what makes your garden special. It's like preparing a stage for a big show where everything needs to be just right. In this part, we'll look at how to check your garden's light, soil, and space to make sure you're ready to create a solid foundation for a thriving pollinator habitat.

Understanding Sunlight Requirements

Sunlight is crucial for your garden because it enables plants to produce food through photosynthesis, benefiting the pollinators that depend on these plants. By watching how sunlight moves across your garden during the day and year, you can understand what will thrive there. Plants needing six hours of sunlight are "full sun" plants, including many that attract pollinators. Less sunny spots suit shade-loving plants. Knowing your garden's sunny and shady areas helps pick plants that will grow best and help pollinators.

Soil Quality and Preparation

Good soil is more than just dirt; it's alive and feeds your garden. Knowing your soil's pH and nutrients helps you make it better for growing. Adding compost can fix poor soil by bringing in beneficial tiny organisms. Also, soil type matters: sandy soil dries quickly, while clay soil can stay too wet, affecting roots. Adjusting your soil for the right mix benefits both plants and their pollinator visitors.

Space Planning

You don't need a big garden to help pollinators; even small spaces like balconies or urban plots can be great for them. Using vertical gardening allows you to grow plants upwards, saving space and providing many flowers for pollinators. Mixing different plants together, known as companion planting, attracts more pollinators by offering a diverse selection. With a bit of creativity, even a tiny garden can become a haven for many kinds of pollinators. Consider the following:

Microclimate Identification

Every garden has its own little climate zones, called microclimates, where different conditions exist for plants to grow. A place that gets sun in the morning but shade in the afternoon could be good for plants that need protection from intense heat. A warm wall might help plants that love heat grow longer. By finding these special spots, you can pick plants that will do well there, making a varied garden that many pollinators will visit. It's all about seeing the unique spots in your garden and using them to boost variety and life.

CHOOSING THE RIGHT LOCATION FOR YOUR POLLINATOR GARDEN

Choosing the best place for your pollinator garden is similar to opening a new cafe; you want a spot that brings in lots of guests, feels welcoming, and is easy for you to look after. We'll look at how to find the best spot that attracts pollinators, fits their needs, and makes the garden enjoyable for both you and the visiting wildlife.

Prioritizing Locations with Maximum Exposure

Attracting pollinators is all about visibility and accessibility. Much like a beacon, your garden needs to stand out:

- Pick spots that are filled with sunlight, which is not just vital for plant health, but is more inviting to pollinators.
- Consider wind exposure. Places with less wind help pollinators navigate and linger. Using a hedge or tall plants can provide protection from the wind without blocking the view.

- Height matters. Using raised beds or elevated planters can help pollinators spot your flowers more easily.

Proximity to Natural Pollinator Habitats

Creating a bridge between the wild and your garden enriches the ecosystem:

- Place your garden close to natural areas or green spaces. These are home to pollinators who will enjoy your garden, too.
- If you're in a city, being near parks or community gardens can help by creating a green chain in the urban area.
- Keep some parts of your garden wild. A spot with local bushes, grass, or a pile of logs can mimic natural habitats, making your garden part of the bigger natural world.

Accessibility for Maintenance

A flourishing garden demands care, making ease of access a practical necessity:

- Pick a place that's close to your tools and water to avoid carrying heavy things too far, which can be tiring.
- Consider the garden's visibility from your home. Not only does this make it easier to enjoy the fruits of your labor, but it also allows you to spot any maintenance needs promptly.
- Adding paths or stepping stones helps you reach all parts of the garden without disturbing the plants or the pollinators.

Consideration for Pollinator Pathways

In the pollinator's view, your garden is like one stop on a much larger map, offering them a place to rest and recharge during their travels.

- By picking the right spot for your pollinator garden and making it friendly for them, you're helping the local environment in a big way.
- The aim is to make a garden that attracts pollinators and is easy for you to take care of, so you can enjoy this lively spot without much trouble.

DESIGN PRINCIPLES FOR POLLINATOR-FRIENDLY GARDENS

Making a garden where pollinators visit, and colors bloom is like creating art. Every plant and color is important. Designing a garden well makes it beautiful and a good home for pollinators. Here, we explore how to design such a sanctuary, focusing on layering, diversity of plants, focal points, seasonal bloom planning, and the strategic use of hardscaping.

Layering and Diversity

Imagine a pollinator buffet spread across different levels of the garden, with dishes ranging from appetizers to desserts, each offering a unique flavor. This is the layering effect that creates a pollinator-friendly garden. This approach involves:

- **Vertical layering**: Using plants of different heights, like low ground covers and tall sunflowers, makes your garden look good in 3D and gives pollinators various places to live and eat.

- **Plant diversity**: Having many kinds of plants, including flowers that bloom every year, bushes, and trees, offers lots of different food sources.
- **Color palette**: Pollinators are drawn to different colors; for example, bees are attracted to blues and purples, while hummingbirds prefer reds. Integrating a rainbow of colors in the garden can attract many different kinds of pollinators.

Creating Focal Points with Native Plants

Native plants are the stars of a pollinator-friendly garden and have evolved to support local wildlife. If you focus on native plants in your garden, you provide essential food to local pollinators like bees and butterflies. These local pollinators are better able to help native plants survive. Consider these steps:

- **Select standout natives**: Pick local plants that pollinators like. These can be plants with big, bright flowers or plants that make a lot of nectar and pollen.
- **Cluster for impact**: Putting local plants together in groups looks good and helps pollinators find their favorite plants more easily. This can even attract pollinators from far away.

Seasonal Bloom Planning

A garden with flowers that bloom in each season gives pollinators food all year. This continuous food source is critical, especially in early spring and late fall when food may be scarce. To achieve this:

- **Early bloomers**: Add plants that bloom early in the spring to provide a crucial food source for pollinators emerging from hibernation.
- **Summer abundance**: During the hot months, make sure you have plants that keep blooming to feed many different pollinators.
- **Late bloomers**: When it starts to get colder, have plants that bloom late into fall to help pollinators prepare for winter or fuel their migration journey.

Incorporating Hardscaping for Shelter

In a pollinator garden, besides plants, hardscaping elements like rocks, logs, and spots of bare ground are very helpful. They give pollinators a place to hide from predators and the elements, to live, and sometimes to get important minerals or salts for their health. You can add these features to your garden in a way that looks good and is useful:

- **Rocks and logs**: If you place elements like rocks and logs carefully, they can become resting spots for butterflies and bees. Over time, these spots will become part of the garden's natural life.
- **Bare soil**: Many local bees make their homes in the soil and need untouched ground. Leaving a small part of your garden wild can give them essential, safe places to nest.
- **Water features**: A shallow water spot, like a bird bath with rocks to land on, gives pollinators the water they need and a spot to cool down.

Designing a garden that helps pollinators is a mix of being creative and caring for nature. It combines making things look beautiful with supporting wildlife. By planning and putting these ideas into action, your garden can grow into a vibrant, pollinator-friendly sanctuary.

SEASONAL PLANNING FOR YEAR-ROUND POLLINATOR SUPPORT

Building a garden that supports pollinators throughout the year involves careful planning and thought. This section will guide you through creating a garden that provides continuous food for pollinators and how to support them when flowers are not in bloom.

Year-Round Blooming Schedules

To ensure the garden stays vibrant and welcoming from the early days of spring to the late moments of fall, choosing the right types of plants is key. It's like organizing a relay race where each plant hands off to the next, keeping a steady stream of flowers going.

Spring: Start with early flowers such as **crocus** and **snowdrops**. They let pollinators know food is coming.

Crocus

Snowdrops

Summer: Fill your garden with colorful flowers like **lavender** and **bee balm** to attract many pollinators.

Lavender

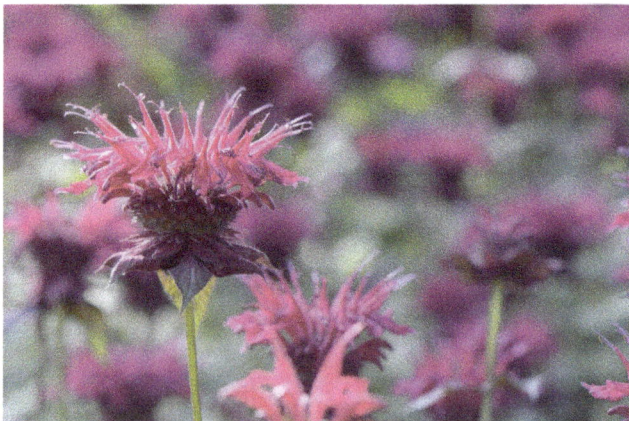

Bee Balm

Fall: Use late bloomers like **goldenrod** and **aster** to feed pollinators as they prepare for winter or migration.

Goldenrod

Aster

Winter Support Strategies

Winter might seem like a quiet time, but pollinators are still struggling to survive. If we plan well, our gardens can be a safe habitat for them during these cold months.

- **Leave the cleanup**: Don't clean up everything in the fall. Letting dead plants and leaves stay can give insects and birds places to find food and shelter.
- **Install habitats**: Consider putting in bug hotels or piles of sticks, which can be safe spots for pollinators to sleep through winter or hide from the cold.
- **Plant evergreens**: Growing evergreen bushes and trees gives pollinators protection all year from weather and predators.

Adjusting for Climate Variability

Our weather has a mix of usual and unexpected patterns. If you adjust your garden plans for these changes, it can still be a welcoming place for pollinators, even when the weather is unpredictable.

- **Stay observant**: Pay attention to weather forecasts and past weather trends. Unexpected cold snaps or very warm winters can change when plants bloom and when pollinators come around.
- **Flexible planting**: Pick plants for your garden that can adapt to weather changes. Some plants can adjust when they flower based on the weather, which helps provide steady food for pollinators.
- **Water wisely**: Make sure your garden gets enough water, especially during very dry periods. A garden that's watered well has a better chance of supporting flowers and pollinators.

Monitoring and Adapting the Garden

A garden is a living, breathing entity, constantly evolving in response to its inhabitants and the environment. Keeping an eye on your garden and making changes to its setup helps it meet the needs of visiting pollinators.

- **Keep a garden diary:** Write down which plants do well, which don't, and what kinds of pollinators visit. Garden diaries are invaluable to have for future planning.
- **Be inventive:** Test out new plants or change your garden layout. Even a little tweak might make your garden more inviting to pollinators.
- **Engage with the community**: Sharing tips and stories with others can give you new ideas and help solve gardening problems.

As the seasons change, our gardens can play a vital role in pollinator survival. By choosing the right plants for food all year and giving them shelter in winter, everything we do can help these important animals survive and thrive. By watching, changing things as needed, and being creative, we can make gardens that are beautiful and also important places for pollinators to live and grow.

INCORPORATING WATER SOURCES FOR POLLINATORS

Importance of Water Sources for Pollinators

Water is essential not just for us and plants, but for small pollinators too, for drinking and sometimes breeding. However, with natural water sources becoming scarce, especially in urban areas, our gardens can offer a lifeline. Next we explore how adding features like bird baths to our gardens can provide needed resources for pollinators and also enhance the appearance of our gardens.

Creating Simple Water Features

Adding a water feature to your garden doesn't have to be complex or expensive. With a little creativity, you can craft safe, accessible spots for pollinators to hydrate:

Bird Bowl

Shallow Baths: Fill shallow bowls or terracotta plant saucers with water and add some stones or marbles, giving pollinators a place to land and drink safely.

Maintaining Water Features

It's very important to keep these water spots clean and safe. If you don't take care of them, the water features can become breeding grounds for diseases. Doing regular maintenance makes sure they stay helpful for pollinators.

- **Regular Cleaning**: Replace the water every few days to stop algae from growing and diseases from spreading. Clean the surfaces well to make sure the water stays clean.
- **Prevent Mosquito Breeding**: Don't let water sit still. If you have a big water feature like a pond, think about adding fish that eat mosquito larvae or using a safe larvicide that doesn't hurt pollinators.
- **Winter Care**: In regions where it gets very cold, take away or empty out water features to stop ice damage. If you keep any water features out all year, make sure they don't

freeze and can still be used by pollinators that are active in winter.]

Placement Considerations

Putting water features in the right spots can ensure their success. Here are some tips to maximize their impact:

- **Visibility**: Put water features near flowers so pollinators can easily find both nectar and water.
- **Shade and Sun**: Having water in both sunny and shady places lets pollinators pick the water temperature they like. Warm water is nice on cold days, and cool spots are great when it's hot.
- **Away from Pesticides**: Keep water away from where you use pesticides or fertilizers, as even small amounts of these can hurt pollinators.

By carefully setting up and keeping water features in our gardens, we give pollinators what they need and make our gardens a welcoming place for them. This makes our gardens full of life and attractive. The water spots are useful and beautiful, drawing in both people and pollinators to enjoy the space.

THE IMPORTANCE OF SHELTER AND NESTING SITES

Making a garden for pollinators is more than just having colorful flowers and places full of nectar. It's about creating a space that mimics their natural habitats, where they can find food, shelter, and nesting sites. Understanding the different kinds of homes pollinators need is important in planning your garden.

Types of Shelters and Nesting Sites

Pollinators, ranging from the tiniest bees to fluttering butterflies and chirping birds, have different requirements when it comes to a garden habitat:

- **Bees:** Some bees like hollow plant stems or holes in wood for laying eggs. Bumblebees prefer soft soil or old mouse nests for their homes.
- **Butterflies** need safe spots to metamorphosis from caterpillars into butterflies, usually in thick leaves or specific host plants that the caterpillars will feed on.
- **Birds**: Birds need safe places to nest and raise their babies, like in trees, bushes, or birdhouses, where they can rear their young away from predators.

Natural vs. Artificial Shelters

Choosing between natural and artificial shelters in a garden often involves thinking about how they look, how well they work, and their effect on the environment.

Natural Shelters: Utilizing plant materials like dense shrubs, grasses, and fallen leaves gives pollinators authentic nesting sites. These materials naturally blend in with your garden and help the soil as it decomposes.

- **Pros:** Eco-friendly, helps many different pollinators, and enhances garden aesthetics.
- **Cons:** Might need more space and take longer to establish.

Artificial Shelters: Installing nesting boxes, bee hotels, and bird-houses gives pollinators a place to stay immediately. These structures can be tailored to the needs of specific species and easily placed throughout the garden.

- **Pros:** Immediate solution, easy to install and monitor, and can be educational.
- **Cons:** It requires maintenance and might not attract as many different pollinators as you would hope to receive.

Placement and Protection

Strategically placing shelters throughout the garden can help pollinators find them and use them safely:

- **Elevation:** Some pollinators, like bees, prefer to have their homes up high. Putting bee hotels or birdhouses on poles or attached to trees or other features can protect them from predators and keep them dry.
- **Orientation:** Placing shelters where they receive morning sun but are protected from intense afternoon sunlight will keep them warm without getting too hot.
- **Vegetation Cover:** Having lots of plants around shelters helps hide them from predators and bad weather, making these places more attractive to pollinators.

Maintenance of Nesting Sites

To keep these shelters safe for pollinators, they need regular care:

- **Cleaning**: Structures like birdhouses and bee hotels should be thoroughly cleaned every year to stop diseases. Do this in late winter or early spring before new pollinators arrive.
- **Repair**: Look for any damage and fix or replace the shelters to keep them safe.

- **Monitoring**: Watch shelters to note which pollinators are using them, which will help you decide what shelters to add or change later.

Using a variety of natural and artificial shelters designed for different pollinators, gardeners can build a garden that supports these essential insects and makes the garden healthier. Carefully choosing where to place these shelters and keeping them in good condition means they'll be safe and welcoming places for a long time, helping your garden and the pollinators thrive.

AVOIDING COMMON PLANNING MISTAKES

Gardening to support pollinators such as bees and butterflies is a valuable and educational goal. However, it's easy to make mistakes while trying to create the ideal environment for them. Let's explore how to sidestep these common pitfalls.

Over-reliance on Exotic Plants

We might love exotic plants for their unique looks, but they often don't meet the needs of our local pollinators, acting more like pretty but useless decorations. Choosing local plants is more advisable because they can feed and shelter native bees and butter-flies. You don't have to give up a beautiful garden; many native plants are just as striking and can make your garden a vibrant, life-filled place.

Ignoring Plant Hardiness Zones

Seeing a plant do well in a friend's garden who lives far away might make us forget about our area's weather. The USDA Plant Hardiness Zones help us know which plants will do best in our regions based on how cold it can get. If we choose plants that don't fit our zone, we might disappoint the pollinators in our garden.

They could be attracted to any flowers that bloom but then find those plants can't survive in our climate, leaving them without food. Choosing plants native to your zone means they'll grow, thrive, and create a reliable place for local pollinators.

Inadequate Plant Diversity

Think of going to a restaurant that only has one meal to offer. That's similar to what pollinators experience in gardens that don't have a mix of plants. Different pollinators need different foods, which they can't get if all the plants are identical. A garden with various plants means something is always blooming, and food is available from the start of spring to the end of fall. This mix also strengthens the garden, making it less susceptible to pests or diseases targeting a specific plant. Adding many varieties of plants helps feed all kinds of pollinators and keeps the garden healthy.

Forgetting about Maintenance Needs

A garden grows and changes, needing regular care to prosper. Watching out for bugs or diseases in plants and dealing with these issues quickly can stop bigger problems later. Including garden upkeep in your daily habits keeps your garden in good shape and strengthens your connection to the garden and the animals it helps.

CREATING A GARDEN THAT GROWS WITH YOU AND THE POLLINATORS

Being flexible is critical to a great garden and for gardeners. As gardens change, we should also change how we look after them, meaning we should be open to learning and growing with the garden. It's about watching, responding, and planning to ensure the garden and its creatures do well.

Adaptive Gardening Practices

Adapting to gardening means paying attention to what your garden needs and being ready to change your plans when those needs change. This change could be as easy as switching out a plant that's not doing well with one that might, or as big as changing part of your garden to deal with more or less sun and shade. The important thing is to see these changes not as mistakes but as chances to make your garden more varied and robust. Here are some tips on how to be flexible in your gardening:

- Keep checking on your plants and pollinators to see how they're doing.
- Be ready to change out plants or rearrange your garden to fit the changing surroundings.
- Try new plants or ways of gardening to make a better home for pollinators.

Building a Resilient Ecosystem

A resilient garden can withstand and bounce back from its challenges, whether environmental pressures, pests, or diseases. Making a resilient garden means focusing on diversity in the plants you grow and the habitats you provide. This diversity creates a more stable ecosystem that can handle disturbances and help a range of pollinators. Here are some ways to make your garden stronger:

- Plant a wide variety of native plants, which tend to be more resistant to local pests and diseases.
- Encourage natural predators in your garden, such as ladybugs and birds, to help keep pest populations in check.

- Practice crop rotation and companion planting to deter pests and improve soil health naturally.

Documenting and Celebrating Success

Keeping a record of your garden's progress is a personal reminder of your journey and an invaluable tool for planning and improvement. Celebrating all wins, no matter the size, shows how your gardening efforts are helping pollinators. Consider these practices:

- Keep a garden journal detailing planting dates, bloom times, and visitor sightings.
- Take regular photos to document the evolution of your garden through the seasons.
- Share your successes with the community through social media, community meetings, or informal garden tours.

Every action we take in our gardens, big or small, helps pollinators and our environment. When we change and improve our gardening ways and make our gardens more resilient, we're helping the whole ecosystem. Sharing what we do with others makes an even more significant difference. Documenting the journey shows us how far we've come and what we still need to do.

4

NATIVE PLANTS - THE UNSUNG HEROES OF POLLINATOR GARDENS

> *"No occupation is so delightful to me as the culture of the earth, and no culture comparable to that of the garden."*
>
> — *THOMAS JEFFERSON*

Think of your garden as a place that changes its offerings with the seasons, using plants that grow well in your area. These plants attract pollinators, just like good food draws people. By choosing native plants for your garden, you're picking the types of plants that local wildlife loves and that are also best adapted to your area's climate and soil, helping them thrive.

THE POWER OF NATIVE PLANTS IN POLLINATOR GARDENS

Ecosystem Harmony

Native plants are the backbone of any thriving pollinator garden. They've spent centuries adapting to their local environment, making them a perfect fit for the garden's microclimate and soil. It's as if these plants are custom-made for the local climate, including rain, temperature changes, and pests. This harmony makes the garden stable and healthy, reducing the need for extra water, fertilizers, and pesticides.

Supporting Local Wildlife

A garden that uses native plants acts like a magnet for pollinators, offering them food and a place to stay. For birds, it's a nesting spot and a food supply. For small animals, it's a haven and a source of food. All these interactions form a detailed network that boosts and adds to the local variety of life.

Reduced Maintenance Needs

Choosing native plants is like getting a skilled chef who's excellent with local ingredients. These plants are good at keeping pests away and do well in the local soil, so you don't need to use as many chemicals. They're used to the local rain and usually don't need extra watering, which is better for the environment, making your garden a green choice.

Enhancing Genetic Diversity

Putting many different native plants in your garden gives pollinators food from spring to fall, similar to how a diverse menu appeals to different tastes. This variety helps support pollinators and wildlife, making the local environment healthier. By selecting and caring for native plants, gardeners can create a thriving spot that benefits pollinators, wildlife, and the community.

REGION-SPECIFIC PLANT GUIDES: NORTHEASTERN U.S.

In the diverse landscape of American gardens, the Northeastern U.S. is unique with its clear-cut seasons, each offering its own set of beauties and hurdles for pollinator-friendly spaces. This region, characterized by its chilly winters and muggy summers, requires hardy plants that can flourish in such varying conditions. We'll look into how the native plants of the Northeast have evolved to suit the local weather and become the top choices for area pollinators, keeping the garden lively all year round.

Adaptation to the Climate

Over thousands of years, the native plants of the Northeastern U.S. have changed to handle the area's weather. They've found ways to survive the cold winters and return to life in warmer seasons. For example, the **Goldenrod** (Solidago spp.) saves energy when it's cold and grows quickly when it gets warm again, giving bees and butterflies nectar in the late season. Likewise, native ferns and smaller plants help protect against heavy rain and offer a cool place in the summer, assisting insects and pollinators.

Pollinator Favorites

Several native plants stand out for their attractiveness to Northeastern pollinators:

New England Aster (Symphyotrichum novae-angliae): With its vibrant purple blooms, this aster is a late-summer beacon for bees and butterflies, offering a rich source of nectar when many other plants have faded.

New England Aster

Joe-Pye Weed (Eutrochium purpureum): Towering and majestic, Joe-Pye Weed's pinkish-purple flowers are a favorite among butterflies. They provide both a food source and a stunning visual highlight.

Joe-Pye Weed

Mountain Mint (Pycnanthemum virginianum): This hardy plant is a powerhouse, attracting an array of pollinators with its nectar-rich flowers and aromatic leaves that deter pests.

Mountain Mint

Wild Columbine (Aquilegia canadensis): With its unique, bell-shaped flowers, Wild Columbine is particularly appealing to hummingbirds, offering a critical food source in early spring.

Wild Columbine

Seasonal Considerations

Having a garden with plants that flower at different times is essential for providing pollinators with continuous food sources all year. From the **Spring Beauty** (Claytonia virginica) that blooms early to the **Witch Hazel** (Hamamelis virginiana) that flowers into winter, each plant helps feed pollinators through the seasons. This way, the garden stays colorful and busy from the start of spring to the beginning of winter and helps keep the pollinators going.

Spring Beauty

Witch Hazel

Ecosystem Benefits

Native plants in the Northeast do much for the environment besides helping pollinators. Their deep roots soak up rainwater, reducing water runoff and soil erosion, which is helpful in places that get a lot of rain or are close to water and could have erosion problems. These plants also help hold the soil together and offer homes and food for many animals, making a well-balanced environment where every creature, big or small, can thrive.

By picking the right native plants, gardeners in the Northeast can make beautiful gardens all year and help the local environment. Choosing plants that fit the climate, bloom in different seasons, and help the ecosystem makes these gardens an essential part of the area, supporting pollinators and other wildlife.

REGION-SPECIFIC PLANT GUIDES: SOUTHEASTERN U.S.

The Southeastern U.S. is rich in warmth, moisture, and bright native plants. This sunny and often humid place has a unique climate that influences the growth of its plants and the pollinators that rely on them. Here, we'll see how the tough native plants of the Southeast are essential helpers for local pollinators, tackle environmental problems, and keep the area's unique cultural background alive.

Heat and Humidity Tolerance

The Southeast has hot summers and mild winters, so plants must handle a lot of sun and moisture. Native plants in this area have evolved to deal well with these conditions. They might have deep roots to find water deep in the ground or leaves with special coatings or tiny hairs to keep water in. These features help them stay healthy and keep flowering, even in scorching weather, ensuring that pollinators always have essential resources.

Highlighting Key Species

Several native plants stand out for their ability to support pollinators while showcasing the beauty and resilience of Southeastern flora:

Swamp Milkweed (Asclepias incarnata): Milkweed, able to thrive in wet environments, is a lifeline for monarch butterflies, offering both a place to lay their eggs and a source of nourishment for their caterpillars.

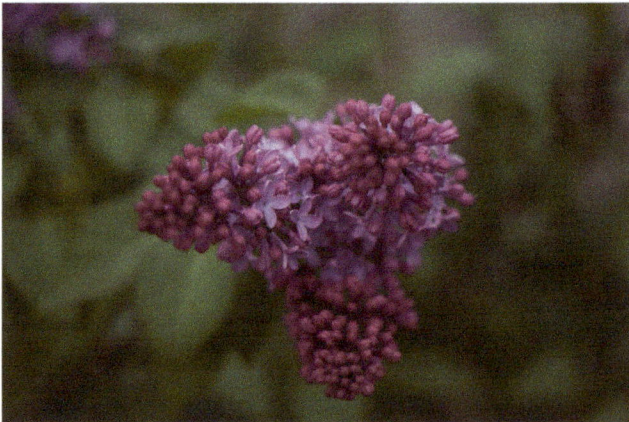

Swamp Milkweed

Southern Magnolia (Magnolia grandiflora): With its large, fragrant flowers, the Southern Magnolia is a beacon for beetles and other pollinators, while its dense foliage provides shelter from the heat.

Southern Magnolia

Purple Coneflower (Echinacea purpurea): This hardy perennial attracts a variety of pollinators, from bees to butterflies, with its nectar-rich blooms and serves as a staple in many Southeastern gardens.

Purple Cornflower

Bottlebrush Buckeye (Aesculus parviflora): Its long, white flower spikes are irresistible to butterflies and bees alike, making it a dynamic focal point in any garden.

Bottlebrush Buckeye

Addressing Local Challenges

Pollinators in the Southeast face many challenges, from habitat loss due to urban expansion to competition for resources with non-native species. Native plant gardens can serve as vital refuges, offering pockets of habitat where pollinators can find food and shelter. By choosing plants adapted to the local environment, gardeners can create low-maintenance landscapes requiring fewer resources and are more resilient to the pressures of urbanization. Moreover, these gardens can help pollinators move quickly across the landscape.

Cultural Significance

Southeastern native plants are essential for the environment and carry the area's rich cultural heritage. Plants like the **Southern Magnolia** (Magnolia grandiflora) symbolize the South's enduring charm and resilience. The **Cherokee Rose** (Rosa laevigata) has historical relevance, with stories tied to the history of the region's indigenous people and early settlers. By growing these plants, we help pollinators and celebrate and keep alive the cultural stories these plants represent.

Cherokee Rose

A garden in the Southeast filled with native plants does more than grow flowers. It reflects the local environment, helps pollinators, and shares the region's stories. By choosing these plants carefully, we do more than make our gardens attractive; we help our planet and preserve our cultural history.

REGION-SPECIFIC PLANT GUIDES: MIDWESTERN U.S.

In the heartland of America, the Midwest is a tapestry of diverse ecosystems, each special in its own way and facing its own challenges. Prairies share our history, tall forests hold old wisdom, and the extreme seasons test the strength of all living things. The native plants thriving here are more than survivors; they feed pollinators, support entire ecosystems, and adapt to the region's varying weather.

Diverse Ecosystems

The Midwest's ecological diversity is a marvel. There are tallgrass prairies filled with native grasses and wildflowers, and dense forests alive with majestic trees, habitats to wildlife and pollinators:

Prairies: Prairies, with their many types of grasses and flowers, are a pollinator's paradise. Plants like the **Prairie Blazing Star** (Liatris pycnostachya) stand tall, and their blooms are a beacon to bees and butterflies.

Prairie Blazing Star

Forests: The shaded woodlands offer a different palette, with flowers like **Wild Geranium** (Geranium maculatum) under the trees and bright **Red Columbine** (Aquilegia canadensis) at the forest's edge.

Wild Geranium

Red Columbine

Pollinator Support

The native flora of the Midwest plays a critical role in sustaining local pollinators, offering them food, shelter, and nesting sites. A very popular standout is:

Purple Coneflower (Silphium laciniatum): A magnet for bees and butterflies, the Purple Cornflower's broad petals and raised centers provide the perfect landing pads for nectar and pollen seekers.

Purple Cornflower

Climate Resilience

Midwestern plants have evolved to withstand the region's climate extremes, from frigid winters to blistering summers and even the occasional flood or drought. They have deep roots that keep the ground in place and find water when it's dry. Their growth matches the changing seasons. These plants are not only resilient but capable of supporting pollinators through varying conditions:

Switchgrass (Panicum virgatum): Switchgrass (Prairie Grass) can grow well in both wet and dry ground, showing it's tough enough to handle the Midwest's changing weather.

New England Aster (Symphyotrichum novae-angliae): This flower blooms late in the season, providing a crucial nectar source when other flowers have faded.

New England Aster

Supporting Migratory Species

The Midwest is important for migrating animals, offering resting and feeding spots vital for survival. Native plants play a primary role in helping wildlife on their migratory journey:

Milkweed

Milkweeds (Asclepias spp.): Milkweeds are crucial for monarch butterflies, giving food to their caterpillars and nectar for the adults during migration.

Sunflowers (Helianthus annuus): Attract a variety of birds, providing seeds that are an essential food source as they prepare for their long journeys.

Sunflower

Midwest gardens, with their diversity of native plants, aren't just pretty. They're essential for supporting many pollinators, offering food and shelter year-round, and helping migrating animals. These plants are strong because they've adapted to the Midwest's harsh weather, making the garden a safe and joyful place through all seasons.

REGION-SPECIFIC PLANT GUIDES: WESTERN U.S.

The Western U.S. features a variety of environments, from deserts to lush valleys and from low plains to high mountains. Here, water-wise gardening is essential and part of the natural way of life. This region's native plants have learned to survive in harsh conditions with little water and thrive.

Water-wise Gardening

In the Western U.S., where water is scarce, gardening must adapt to this reality. Local plants are experts at surviving with minimal water, reaching deep or wide with their roots to capture any available moisture. They guide us in water-wise gardening, encouraging us to work with the environment rather than fight it. By using mulch, preparing the soil properly, and setting up efficient watering systems, we support these plants' natural ways, cutting down on extra watering. In this manner, we can create a garden that reflects the toughness of the West's natural landscapes.

Diverse Plant Recommendations

The Western U.S. is a land of contrasts, from the coastal breezes to the desert sun. Its native plants fit the varied landscapes they live in:

Coastal Areas: The **Seaside Paintbrush** (Castilleja affinis) (also known as Indian Paintbrush) thrives in sandy soil and doesn't mind the salt in the air.

Seaside (Indian) Paintbrush

Mountain Ranges: The **Rocky Mountain Penstemon** (Penstemon strictus) and the **Colorado Blue Columbine** (Aquilegia caerulea) bring vibrant colors to higher altitudes, matching the sky.

Rocky Mountain Penstemon

Colorado Blue Columbine

Deserts: The **Desert Marigold** (Baileya multiradiata) and **Joshua Tree** (Yucca brevifolia) are great examples of desert toughness, showing how to survive with little water.

Desert Marigold

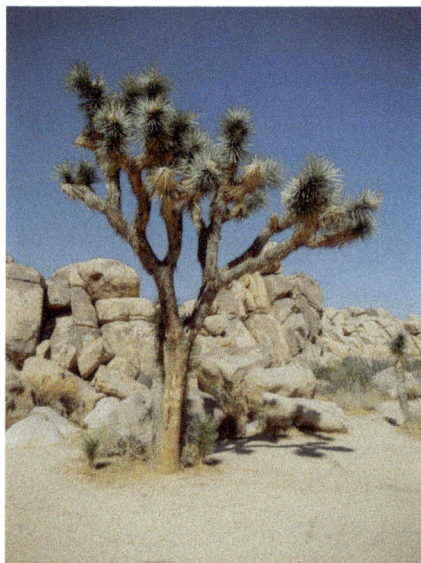

Joshua Tree

Each of these plants helps complete the environmental big picture by providing nectar and pollen for pollinators. They also show the unique natural history of their region.

Fire Resistance

In the Western U.S., fires are a natural part of ecosystems, helping new plants grow. But we are trying to lower this fire risk in our gardens. Luckily, many local plants can resist fire. They have moist or thick leaves that protect them from fire, and their deep roots keep the soil stable and reduce erosion after

California Poppy

a fire. Plants like the **California Poppy** (Eschscholzia californica) and **Soap Plant** (Chlorogalum pomeridianum) are not only pretty, they help make gardens better prepared for fires. Adding these plants makes your garden safer and keeps in mind the area's fire patterns.

Soap Plant

Pollinator Corridors

The large open areas in the West can be challenging for pollinators due to the significant habitat gaps. Creating "pollinator corridors," paths of native plants connecting these spaces, can help. These corridors act like highways for pollinators, giving them places to rest and feed. This strategy effectively links isolated green areas into a network that supports habitat health. Gardeners can contribute by planting native species, helping to form a network that promotes pollinators across vast distances, which is crucial for their survival and the health of the land.

In the Western U.S., a well-thought-out garden can be a haven for people and wildlife, overcoming the region's challenges. These gardens offer shelter and help to local pollinators, acting as oases in dry areas, warm spots in cold mountains, and beacons in coastal fog.

REGION-SPECIFIC PLANT GUIDES: SOUTHWESTERN U.S.

In the Southwestern U.S., nature shows its resilience and vibrant color. Native plants are masters at living in an environment with lots of sun and little rain. This section addresses how these plants adapt, look beautiful, and are helpful, allowing you to select plants that will flourish and make your garden a haven for pollinators and a reflection of the area's culture.

Adaptation to Arid Environments

Southwest native plants are experts at living in dry areas. They've devised ways to save water and be efficient at making food through photosynthesis. **Succulents** hold water in their big leaves, while plants like **Sagebrush** have small, shiny leaves to keep water from evaporating. Their roots go deep or spread out to find water, helping them survive long, dry periods. These tough qualities make them perfect for creating vibrant gardens that need little water and attract pollinators.

Succulents

Sagebrush

Key Species for Pollinators

Agave (Agave americana): With its striking form, the **Agave** is not just an architectural marvel but a crucial nectar source for bats, acting as a keystone species in the desert's pollination network.

Agave

Penstemon (Penstemon utahensis): The vibrant spikes of **Penstemon** attract a variety of bees and hummingbirds, and its many species offer bright colors to the arid landscape.

Penstemon

Cultural and Historical Uses

The Southwest is full of stories tied to local plants. These plants are more than just desert survivors; they are integral to the identity and traditions of the region's indigenous peoples and early settlers. The tapestry of the Southwest is rich with cultural narratives, many of which are woven with threads of native plant lore.

Yucca (Yucca filamentosa): Beyond its striking appearance, **Yucca** holds a revered place in Native American culture. It is used in ceremonies and as a source of fiber, food, and medicine.

Yucca

Cholla (Cylindropuntia): The fruit of the **Cholla** cactus, despite its protective spines, has been a traditional food. Its flowers are also a crucial food source for desert pollinators.

Cholla Cactus Flower

Adding these plants to your garden helps the environment and keeps the Southwest's history and culture alive, linking us to the land and its past.

Conservation and Water Use

In regions where water is scarce, using native plants is imperative. Gardeners who choose plants that naturally grow in their area will use less water, contributing to the sustainability of the area's water resources. Plus, planting these native species will support local wildlife by offering them habitats, even as natural landscapes are being divided up.

Prickly Pear Cactus (Opuntia): Its ability to thrive with minimal water makes it a symbol of water-wise gardening, its flowers a magnet for insects, and its fruit for birds.

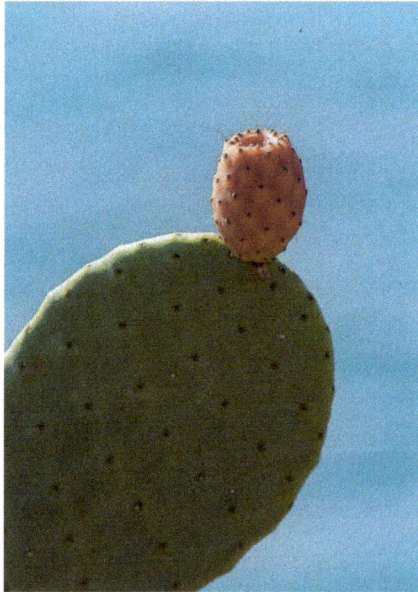

Prickly Pear Cactus

Mesquite (Prosopis): The deep roots of the mesquite tree tap into hidden water reserves, its canopy offers shade, and its pods provide food for a variety of wildlife.

Mesquite Tree

In the Southwest's gardens, every plant has a story of getting by in tough places and still being beautiful. These local plants are vital for helping pollinators and connect us to the area's land and culture. Choosing these plants means we're creating gardens that are not just nice to look at but also full of the life and traditions of the Southwest.

HOW TO SOURCE AND SELECT HEALTHY PLANTS

When we want to fill our gardens with plants that help local pollinators, choosing and finding these plants is just as important as caring for them. This section shows how to pick the right plants carefully to help our local environment and ensure we don't accidentally harm the garden by introducing invasive species.

Local Nurseries and Garden Centers

Finding a nursery or garden center that stocks various native plants isn't just a shopping trip; it's an investment in the local ecosystem. These nurseries often have staff who understand the regional climate and soil conditions, making them invaluable resources. They can help you choose native plants best suited to your area and climate and how they contribute to supporting local wildlife, including pollinators.

- Visit nurseries that specialize in native plants or those that have a dedicated section for them.
- Check out your area's plant sales or garden fairs, often hosted by gardening clubs or environmental organizations.
- Engage with the staff to ask about the plants' origin and their benefits to pollinators. Their knowledge can help you choose plants that do well in your area.

Inspecting Plants for Health

Choosing a healthy plant helps support pollinators a lot. Here's what to check:

- Make sure the leaves are bright green, showing the plant's health. Yellow or spotted leaves could mean it's diseased.
- Examine the stem and underside of leaves for signs of pests. Healthy plants should be free from visible insects or damage caused by them.
- If you can, look at the roots. They should be white or light and spread well in the pot, not too tightly wound up.

Supporting Local Ecosystems

- Choosing local plants for your garden does more than make it look nice; it's a vital part of the local environment. These plants have evolved with the local pollinators, birds, and insects, forming partnerships vital for a healthy ecosystem.
- Before buying, make sure the plants you're interested in are native to your area and help local pollinators.
- Think about plants that serve multiple purposes in the ecosystem, such as providing homes and food for pollinators and other animals.
- Choose various plants that bloom at different times of the year so pollinators have a continuous food source.

Avoiding Invasive Species

While exotic plants are attractive, their impact on local ecosystems can be detrimental. Many exotic species are invasive and can overpower native plants, monopolizing resources and throwing off the natural balance of local habitats.

- Familiarize yourself with the list of invasive species in your region. Many states and local conservation groups provide resources to help identify these plants.
- Consult with local experts or extension services if you need clarification on a plant.
- Carefully remove any invasive species you might already have in your garden, ensuring they are disposed of properly so they won't spread further.

DIGITAL TOOLS FOR PLANT IDENTIFICATION

With developments in technology, you can now choose from several plant identification apps that can help in your garden. These apps will help you select plants to add to your garden and identify plants you already have. Using a plant app is incredibly helpful when monitoring any weed growth. Here are some of the top plant identification apps you can use:

- **PlantNet**: This free-to-use app might be considered a science project on biodiversity. You can download it on either iOS or Android gadgets. The app covers 20,000 plant species from around the world. It also identifies whether the plant is ornamental or cultivated. You can use PlantNet by sharing an image of the plant you want to identify. Make sure that the photo you share is of good quality and positioned well. The app will tell you the name of the plant and similar plants so you can verify if it is the correct plant identification. Other users can also verify the plant identification.
- **iNaturalist**: This is also free to use. It is a joint initiative of the National Geographic Society and the California Academy of Science. Some contributors record their sightings in the app's database. Other users and image recognition technology verify the app's plant identification feature. The app also has a database of insects, animals, and butterflies, among other species. You can use iNaturalist on iOS or Android devices.
- **PlantSnap**: This app is free to use and provides a digital interface between people and nature. Its database includes over 500,000 species of flowers, ornamental plants, cacti and succulents, and mushrooms. It uses artificial intelligence to identify plants. The user can

upload a photo of a leaf or part of a plant for identification.

Choosing the right plants from the nursery is critical to creating lively gardens with busy pollinators and healthy plants. When we select plants that benefit our local environment, we're doing more than gardening; we're taking care of a part of the world and helping it thrive for future pollinators.

NON-NATIVE PLANTS TO AVOID AND WHY

Not all plant colors match well in gardening. Even if they look beautiful, some colors can upset the garden's balance. Adding plants from other areas without understanding their impact on the local environment can be risky. These plants might become invasive, overpowering local plants and damaging the environment. They often spread fast and are hard to get rid of.

Invasive Species Risks

"**Invasive**" refers to species that spread widely in a new area, causing damage to nature, the economy, or health. Non-native plants can turn invasive if they spread rapidly, reproduce a lot, and have no natural enemies in their new place. This can cause them to take over, leaving native plants without enough food, light, or space. Over time, this reduces the variety of local plants and animals, including those that pollinate plants.

Examples of Problematic Plants

Some non-native plants have become notorious for their invasive tendencies across various regions, creating significant challenges for local wildlife and ecosystems:

Kudzu, initially used to control soil erosion, now covers large areas in the Southeast, overwhelming native trees, shrubs, and other plants.

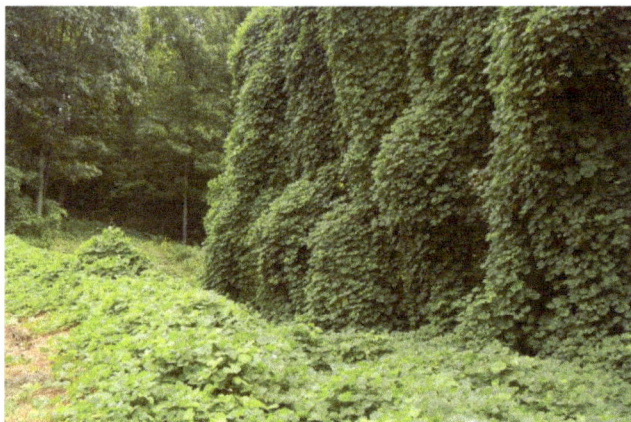

Kudzu

Introduced as an ornamental plant, **purple loosestrife** (Lythrum salicaria) has invaded wetlands across the Northeast and Midwest, displacing native wetland plants crucial for aquatic wildlife.

Purple Loosestrife

English Ivy, famous for decorating, aggressively covers forests in the Pacific Northwest, choking trees and taking over the ground.

English Ivy

Environmental Impact

Invasive plants from other areas can harm the environment by leading to the loss of animal homes and less diversity in nature. When these plants spread, they change the structure of habitats and the essential food sources needed by native wildlife, including pollinators. Fewer native animals and plants result, upsetting the natural balance. Moreover, invasive plants can alter the soil's properties and water flow, posing a challenge to the survival and growth of native plant species.

Following these gardening tips improves the look and health of our gardens and helps preserve and restore local habitats. By avoiding invasive plants, we respect nature's balance and create gardens that live peacefully with the environment.

5

SUSTAINABLE GARDENING PRACTICES

"The first rule of sustainability is to align with natural forces, or at least try not to defy them."

— *PAUL HAWKEN*

Imagine your garden as a safe spot where every plant and method of gardening is chosen to help, not hurt, every visitor. Every choice is about what's natural, healthy, and makes us happy. Organic gardening nurtures life at every level, from tiny organisms in the soil to the pollinators visiting your flowers. It means looking after a bit of the earth so it's secure, full of life, and buzzing with nature.

ORGANIC GARDENING TECHNIQUES FOR POLLINATOR HEALTH

Avoiding Synthetic Chemicals

The first step towards a pollinator-friendly garden is saying no to synthetic pesticides and fertilizers. These chemicals can harm more than just the pests—they can affect helpful bugs, birds, and the soil. For example, chemicals called neonicotinoids can cause bees to decline. Going organic means gardening in a way that works with nature's balance, where every living thing has its place.

- **What to use instead**: Embrace natural pest control methods. Strongly spraying water can remove aphids from roses, and a mix of soap and water can fight off many types of bugs.

Organic Soil Amendment

Healthy soil is the foundation of a thriving garden. Organic matter, such as compost or green manure, enriches the soil, introducing beneficial microbes that help plants absorb nutrients more effectively. This natural approach supports plant growth, which in turn benefits pollinators.

- **Getting started**: Make a compost bin using kitchen leftovers and garden trimmings. This will reduce trash and give your garden a boost of nutrients.

Companion Planting

Companion planting is a natural way to deter pests while improving plant growth, meaning you don't have to do as much work. For instance, planting marigolds in your vegetable garden can keep nematodes and other pests at bay, and growing basil next to tomatoes can make the tomatoes taste better and grow stronger.

- **Try this pairing**: Lavender and rosemary attract bees with their blooms and repel deer and rabbits.
- **Consider** Basil with flowering plants such as borage and marigolds.
- **Also**, using a mix of green, purple, and variegated basil will provide bees with various options.

Certified Organic Plants

Choosing plants grown without artificial pesticides or fertilizers helps your garden start off healthy, ensuring you don't accidentally introduce harmful chemicals into your ecosystem. For edible plants, this is important because chemical leftovers can harm you and the pollinators that come to your garden.

- **Where to find them**: Local farmers' markets, organic nurseries, and even some larger garden centers now offer a selection of certified organic seedlings and seeds.

Organic gardening helps protect pollinators, which are essential for our environment and keeps our planet healthy. It's a way to make our gardens better for all living things and more sustainable.

NATURAL PEST CONTROL: PROTECTING POLLINATORS FROM HARM

Natural pest control and pollinators work together like music. This way of gardening focuses on keeping things balanced instead of trying to remove pests entirely. It respects the complex relationships between plants, pests, and their natural predators. The goal is to guide the natural world gently, creating a space where every form of life can do well.

Identifying Beneficial Insects

A garden full of activity shows it's healthy, with many visitors acting as hidden helpers. These good insects control pests naturally. Knowing who these helpers are is essential to managing pests without chemicals.

Ladybugs: These bright beetles love eating aphids, and one ladybug can eat up to 5,000 aphids in its lifetime.

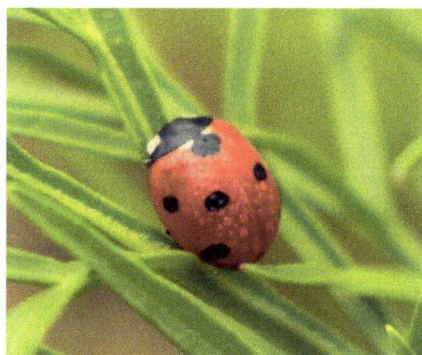

Ladybug

Lacewings: These insects with fine wings are more than pretty. Their larvae, called 'aphid lions,' eat many soft pests.

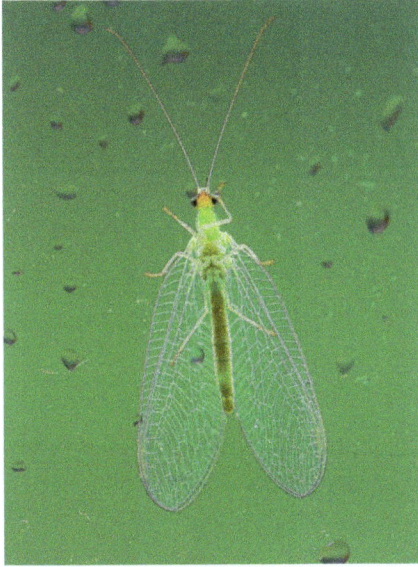

Lacewing

Hoverflies: They look like bees but are great at controlling aphids. Their young are especially good at eating pests.

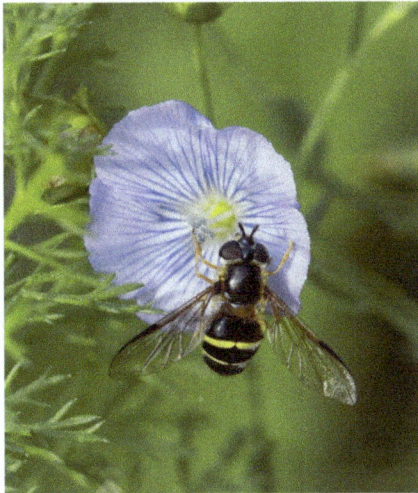

Hoverfly

Understanding what these insects do allows us to support them, creating an ecosystem where they can live and help our gardens.

DIY Pest Control Solutions

When intervention is necessary, natural solutions offer a way to manage pests without harming pollinators or beneficial insects. Following are some natural remedies that you can make with common household ingredients:

- **Soap Spray**: Mixing a little liquid soap with water can keep many pests away. The soap damages the pests' outer skin, stopping infestations naturally.
- **Neem Oil**: This oil comes from the neem tree and is a robust and natural bug killer that works on pests like aphids and mites. If used correctly, it's safe for pollinators.
- **Garlic Spray**: The pungent smell of garlic can drive off many garden pests. Mixing garlic, water, and a bit of soap makes a spray that pests don't like.

Using these methods carefully helps protect your garden in a way that keeps everything balanced.

Physical Barriers

Sometimes, the most effective protection is a barrier—like a fence for gardens, one that stops pests from getting to plants but still lets pollinators pass through.

- **Insect Netting** is a thin mesh that keeps flying and jumping bugs away from plants. It lets light and rain in but keeps pests out.

- **Row Covers** are light cloths that cover plants to protect them from pests and help create a warm environment for better growth. They are great for young plants or when there are a lot of pests.
- **Collars**: For plants at risk from ground pests, like cutworms, a collar made from a cardboard tube or plastic cup can keep them safe.

Employing these barriers can prevent pests from ever becoming a problem.

Timely Intervention

In gardening, responding quickly to pest problems can prevent minor problems from becoming big ones. It is very important to catch pests early and deal with them naturally.

- **Watch Plants Closely**: Paying attention to your plants helps you notice pests as soon as they appear. Early action can make natural methods work better.
- **Act Fast**: When you see pests, figure out what to do quickly. Sometimes, you can remove a few pests by hand or use a simple spray to stop more from coming.
- **Know Pest Cycles**: Understanding when and how pests grow can help you stop them before they spread. For example, using good nematodes in the soil can stop pests like grubs early on.

This method, which involves watching closely and acting fast, prevents small problems from getting bigger and keeps the garden balanced.

Using natural ways to control pests helps keep everything in the garden, from soil microorganisms to busy pollinators, healthy, making our gardens strong, full of life, and buzzing with activity.

MULCHING AND COMPOSTING FOR A HEALTHIER GARDEN

Soil is vital for plant growth and is home to many helpful tiny creatures in a lively garden. Two important ways to help this soil are mulching and composting. Both improve the garden's health and help the pollinators that come to it.

Benefits of Mulching

Mulching, covering the soil with a protective layer of organic or inorganic material, is like giving your garden a warm blanket. Mulching is necessary for many reasons:

- **Moisture retention**: Mulch helps soil retain moisture by reducing evaporation, ensuring that plants—and the pollinators that rely on them—have access to water even during dry spells.
- **Temperature regulation**: Mulch controls the soil's temperature, keeping plant roots protected from extreme heat in summer and cold in winter.
- **Weed suppression**: A layer of mulch can hinder weed growth, reducing competition for plants and less disturbance for pollinators.

Choosing the Right Mulch

Not every mulch is the same, and selecting the right type is crucial for supporting pollinator health:

- **Organic mulches:** Organic mulches like straw, wood chips, and leaves improve the soil as they break down, helping plants and the microorganisms vital to soil health.
- **Inorganic mulches:** Inorganic mulches, like stones or landscape fabric, don't add nutrients but can be suitable for paths around heat-loving plants that need extra warmth.

When using mulch, a layer of 2-3 inches is usually enough. You should not place mulch too close to plant stems.

Composting Basics

Composting turns kitchen scraps and garden waste into valuable soil. This rich, nutrient-dense mix encourages vigorous plant growth and provides a bounty for pollinators.

- **What to compost**: You can compost fruit and veggie scraps, coffee grounds, eggshells, grass, and leaves. However, to avoid attracting pests and spreading diseases, don't compost meat, dairy, or sick plants.
- **Starting your compost pile**: Pick a sunny place for your compost. Layer green materials (like food scraps, for nitrogen) with brown materials (like leaves, for carbon) and keep it damp. Stirring the pile weekly aerates it and helps it break down faster.

Using Compost

Using compost in your garden dramatically benefits your soil, similar to providing a high-quality meal. It offers several advantages:

- **Improving soil structure**: Compost improves the soil's texture, breaking up heavy clay soils making it easier for roots to grow and soils to hold moisture.
- **Enhancing nutrient availability**: Compost slowly releases nutrients, giving plants a balanced diet for solid growth, which benefits pollinators.
- **Supporting soil life**: Compost-enriched soil helps maintain soil health, creating an environment where plants and pollinators can flourish.

To apply compost, spread it over your garden beds in either spring or fall, mixing it into the top few inches of soil, or use it as a surface layer around existing plants.

WATER CONSERVATION STRATEGIES IN THE POLLINATOR GARDEN

Water is crucial for our gardens, just like soil, but it's often used too much or wasted. Saving water is vital in gardens for pollinators. Using water-saving methods helps us use just enough water for the plants that support pollinators without using more than we need.

Drip Irrigation

Drip irrigation is very precise and saves water by delivering it right to the plant's roots, reducing water loss. Although setting up a drip irrigation system is expensive, it saves a lot of water and helps plants grow better. When water is limited, or during droughts, a drip irrigation system is greatly effective, ensuring water is used wisely.

Rainwater Harvesting

Rain doesn't always fall when needed, but saving it can keep our gardens green during droughts. You can collect rainwater simply, like using barrels under downspouts to catch water from your roof. Or, you can make a rain garden, a shallow dip planted with plants that thrive in water, to slow down runoff and let it soak into the earth. Both techniques conserve water and aid in managing stormwater.

Water-wise Gardening

Adopting **water-wise gardening** practices involves planning the garden and its maintenance to ensure the whole garden conserves water. This includes:

- **Choosing drought-tolerant native plants:** Since drought-tolerant plants need less water, choose plants that handle dry conditions well and are native to your area.
- **Utilizing mulch to fight weeds:** Mulch makes the garden look good, helps the soil hold moisture, and cuts down on watering.
- **Improving soil structure:** Adding organic matter to the soil can increase its water-holding capacity, giving plants longer-term access to water.

Using each of these practices in your garden design creates a landscape that is beautiful, resilient, and able to thrive with less water.

Optimal Watering Practices

Watering your garden efficiently can save a lot of water and is better for your plants. Consider these practices:

- **Watering in the early morning**: Watering in the morning ensures more water reaches the plants and stops it from evaporating too quickly. It also keeps plants from getting fungal diseases by not allowing them to remain wet overnight.
- **Using a soaker hose or watering can** directs water where plants need it, at their roots, instead of on the leaves or flowers. This saves water and ensures the plants get water where it helps them the most.
- **Observing your plants** for signs that they require watering, like droopy or changing color leaves, can guide you to water them only when needed, which will avoid watering too much or too little.

Using clever watering methods helps create a garden where every bit of water is used wisely. Smart water use is a key part of gardening that helps our gardens and the pollinators living in them thrive now and in the future.

SEASONAL GARDEN MAINTENANCE TIPS

In the life of a garden, every season brings different needs and tasks. Adapting our care to meet these changing needs ensures our gardens remain vibrant, healthy spaces that continue supporting and attracting pollinators. From spring's first buzz to winter's calm, let's explore how to adjust our gardening practices to the season's needs.

Spring Preparations

As the frost recedes and the first green shoots emerge, our gardens signal a new beginning. Spring is a time of preparation and anticipation, setting the stage for the bustling months ahead.

- **Clearing winter debris**: Start by clearing away dead plants that aren't sheltering animals. This cleanup reduces places where pests and diseases can hide, leading to a healthier garden.
- **Dividing perennials**: The best time to split perennials is early spring before plants start growing fast. This makes plants healthier and gives your garden more flowers for pollinators to visit.
- **Planting early bloomers**: Adding plants that flower early, like crocuses, snowdrops, and hellebores, gives food to pollinators emerging from hibernation. These early flowers are crucial for bridging the gap until more abundant food sources become available.

Summer Care

Summer care focuses on sustaining growth and vibrancy with the garden in full swing, ensuring our plants support various pollinators.

- **Watering wisely**: As it gets hotter, use water efficiently by watering plants deeply but not too often. Deep watering encourages root growth, strengthening plants against heat and drought.
- **Mulching**: New organic mulch keeps the soil wet and roots cool. Over time, the mulch breaks down, making the soil richer for plants and microorganisms.
- **Monitoring for pests and diseases**: Regularly inspect plants for signs of stress or infestation. Finding early issues allows for more gentle, natural interventions and ensures your garden is safe for pollinators.

Fall Cleanup and Planting

As days get shorter and the garden calms down, fall's gardening tasks prepare for winter and set the groundwork for the following year's growth.

- **Planting autumn-blooming plants**: Adding plants like asters and goldenrods that flower in fall gives pollinators a food source late into the year. Having a food source late in the year is crucial for pollinators to get energy for migration to warmer places or surviving the winter.
- **Preparing the garden for winter**: Cut back plants that have finished blooming, leaving any that still provide structure or seeds for birds. Plant spring bulbs for an early start next year.
- **Soil care**: Fall is a great time to improve your soil. Adding compost or leaf mold makes the soil richer and prepares it for planting in the spring.

Winter Considerations

Even when the garden is covered with snow or frost, there are ways to keep it welcoming for wildlife and ready to come back to life in the spring.

- **Leaving some dead material**: You don't need to clean up everything in the fall. Keeping seed heads and some dead plants helps feed birds and shelter insects that stay through winter. These refuges are critical for maintaining a healthy pollinator population.
- **Protecting pollinator habitats**: If you've created habitats like bee hotels or butterfly puddlers, check them for damage and make repairs as needed. Ensure they are safe

from winter winds and positioned to avoid the wettest conditions.

- **Mulching**: Putting down mulch after the ground freezes keeps plants safe from winter's changing temperatures, helps avoid frost damage, and keeps roots stable.

With each seasonal task, our gardens change and build on what came before, making a welcoming place for pollinators throughout the year. This continuous care aligns with nature's patterns, creating a beautiful garden alive with wildlife. As gardeners, we do more than just tend to plants; we are guardians of a larger ecosystem, with every season bringing a new part of our ongoing story.

MANAGING WEEDS WITHOUT HARMING POLLINATORS

Every plant matters in a garden, but some, known as weeds, are only sometimes wanted. How we handle these weeds is important so we don't harm the food source for pollinators. We need to find a way to manage weeds that helps rather than hurts the garden.

Understanding Weeds

Only some weeds are good in the garden. Some, like dandelions and clover, help pollinators by providing nectar and pollen early on. But if they start taking over and upset the balance of the garden, we need to step in. The trick is to figure out which weeds to keep for the pollinators and which to remove.

Dandelion

Dandelions: Often one of the first food sources available to bees in spring.

Clover: Fixes nitrogen in the soil and provides nectar to various pollinators.

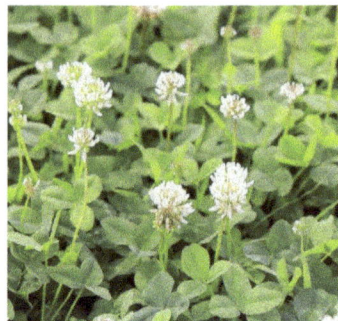

Clover

Dealing with weeds isn't about getting rid of them all. It's about finding a middle ground that keeps the garden looking good and helps the environment.

Manual Removal

Removing weeds by hand or with tools helps remove them without causing too much disruption. This method requires more effort but is accurate, avoiding damage to nearby plant roots and insects. It also keeps the soil undisturbed, protecting ground-nesting pollinators' homes.

- **Early intervention**: Removing weeds when they are small makes the job easier and stops them from spreading seeds.
- **Mindful disturbance**: Carefully loosen the soil around weeds to avoid hurting pollinator larvae and eggs.

Organic Herbicides

Using organic herbicides might work if you can't pull weeds by hand. These are made from natural materials and can kill weeds without harming the environment as much as synthetic chemicals. But you should still be careful. Even natural herbicides can harm other plants and pollinators if not used carefully.

- **Vinegar-based herbicides**: Vinegar-based herbicides work well for targeting specific weeds on sunny days. The acetic acid in them breaks down fast, so they don't harm the environment for long.
- **Corn gluten meal**: Corn gluten meal is a natural herbicide that stops weed seeds from growing. It works best when used along with other weed management programs.

When using organic herbicides, apply them only where needed. Don't cover large areas to avoid harming beneficial plants and insects.

Preventative Strategies

Prevention is the most gentle and effective method of managing weeds, ensuring they don't become a problem in the first place.

- **Ground covers**: Planting ground covers like creeping thyme or phlox helps stop weeds by covering the ground and using up resources. These plants also attract pollinators, supporting the garden in two ways.
- **Mulch**: Organic mulch keeps the soil moist, improves soil health, and blocks sunlight, stopping weed seeds from growing.

By creating a garden where chosen plants thrive, we naturally reduce the chance of weeds appearing. This way, we can have a lively garden that's good for pollinators with minimal need for intervention.

ENCOURAGING NATURAL PREDATORS AND BENEFICIAL INSECTS

Every part of a garden's ecosystem, from tiny insects to bright flowers, is essential. Natural predators and helpful bugs are critical players in keeping the garden balanced and healthy for pollinators. To support these helpful creatures, we must make our gardens welcoming by providing them with homes and food through careful plant selection.

Habitat Creation

Making homes for beneficial insects is like creating a community where each bug, from solitary bees to ladybugs, has its own needs for where to live or hide. Meeting these needs turns your garden into a lively place with helpful insects.

- **Beetle banks**: Beetle banks are raised areas or beds with thick grass that offer great hiding places for ground beetles and spiders. These creatures help control pests in the garden.
- **Insect hotels**: These structures, made from bamboo tubes, wood with holes, and other small spaces, provide homes for solitary bees and wasps. Placing them where it's sunny and close to flowers helps these insects find food quickly.
- **Diverse plantings**: Using a mix of plants with different textures, heights, and flowering times creates an environment that suits the different needs of beneficial insects.

Creating these homes for insects makes the garden healthier and adds interest, encouraging us to watch the intricate ways these creatures interact.

Plant Selection

Choosing the right plants is crucial for attracting beneficial insects. These plants act as a pantry and a haven, offering nectar, pollen, and shelter.

- **Herbs**: Herbs that bloom, such as dill, fennel, and cilantro, draw in many helpful insects like parasitic wasps and hoverflies. The young of these insects are great at eating pests.
- **Native flowers**: Flowers such as goldenrod, aster, and sunflower are magnets for beneficial insects. Their blooms provide a rich source of nectar throughout the seasons.
- **Umbellifers**: Umbellifers, plants with flowers that form an umbrella shape like Queen Anne's lace and yarrow, are very appealing to good insects, providing them with an accessible meal.

Incorporating these plants into the garden ensures a steady stream of natural defenders, ready to enter when pests appear.

Avoiding Broad-Spectrum Pesticides

Broad-spectrum pesticides are like a one-size-fits-all solution in the garden. Unfortunately, they affect both harmful and helpful insects. These chemicals do not discriminate, harming the beneficial insects vital for a healthy garden.

- **Impact on beneficial insects**: These pesticides can stay active for weeks, creating long-term risks for insects that touch them, even those coming from nearby places.
- **Alternatives**: Using specific methods like removing pests

by hand or applying certain organic treatments reduces harm to other, non-problematic species.

Avoiding these pesticides helps protect the complex life network in our gardens, ensuring every creature that visits or lives there finds a safe place.

Understanding the Predator-Prey Balance

The relationship between predators and pests is like a seesaw that needs both sides to be balanced. This balance helps keep the garden healthy by naturally controlling pests.

- **Natural cycles**: Understanding that pest numbers will fluctuate and that helpful predators usually follow these changes can help gardeners better prepare for and handle pest problems.
- **Patience**: Sometimes, allowing a minor pest outbreak to unfold can encourage beneficial insects to move in, addressing the issue naturally.
- **Diversity**: A garden with many diverse plants brings in various helpful insects, preventing any one pest group from taking over.

Embracing this balance means accepting the garden as a living entity, one that self-regulates through its inhabitants' interactions. It's a shift from a mindset of control to cooperation, where every creature, from the smallest insect to the gardener, plays a role in the garden's health.

ADAPTING YOUR GARDEN AS THE CLIMATE CHANGES

Gardening involves both doing and watching, adjusting to the climate's changes. It's about understanding our environment and being open to changing our gardening to fit with nature's signals. As gardeners, we're in a unique place where we can care for the earth and help others learn, mainly as we deal with climate change.

Climate-Resilient Plants

Selecting plants that can thrive under changing climate conditions is like choosing team members who can play well. These resilient plant types can handle very hot and unexpectedly cold weather, ensuring our gardens stay welcoming for pollinators no matter the climate.

Heat-tolerant plants like **lavender** and **sedum** do well in hot weather without drooping, which is ideal for hotter locations.

Lavender

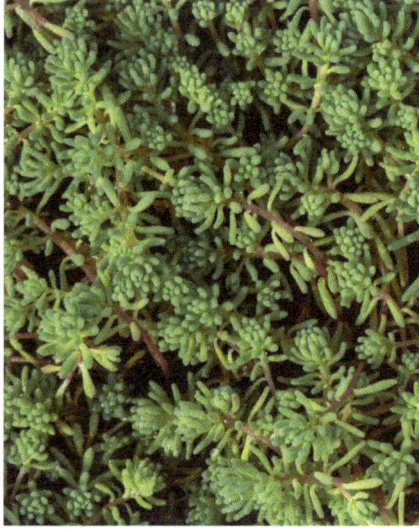

Sedum

Flood-resistant plants like **swamp milkweed** and **Joe-Pye weed** can handle very wet conditions, helping stabilize areas that get a lot of rain or floods.

Swamp Milkweed

Joe-Pye Weed

Drought-adapted plants like **sage** and **ornamental grasses** save water and do well in areas where it's often dry.

Sage

Ornamental Grass

Adding these tough plants to our gardens helps the gardens survive and keeps a steady food supply for pollinators, which is very important during harsh environmental conditions.

Adaptive Garden Design

Creating a garden that can handle climate change isn't just about choosing plants; it's about planning the whole garden, from the soil to places for shelter.

- **Creating microclimates** through strategic planting creates small, controlled climates that can protect sensitive plants from harsh weather. Taller plants are used for shade or barriers to block the wind and keep moisture in.
- **Water-wise techniques** are crucial. Methods like mulching and using efficient watering systems help save water and ensure it gets to the plant roots where it's needed.
- **Flexible layouts** that can be modified as conditions change, like pots you can move or garden beds you can

rearrange, allow you to adjust to different environmental conditions quickly.

These gardening strategies protect our gardens from climate change and turn them into solid ecosystems that can support many pollinators all year round.

Monitoring and Responding

Paying attention to our gardens and their living creatures helps us make intelligent choices and adjust our care to suit their changing needs.

- **Regular observations** of plant growth, their flowering times, and the activity of pollinators help us understand the effects of climate change by noticing shifts in patterns or possible problems.
- **Seasonal adjustments** such as adjusting planting times, how often we water, and how we maintain our gardens each season can help deal with weather changes, keeping our gardens flourishing.
- **Responsive actions** like introducing heat-tolerant plant varieties in warmer temperatures or improving drainage to combat heavier rainfall show our commitment to sustainably caring for our gardens and the planet.

This active engagement with our gardens not only strengthens them but also strengthens our bond with nature, creating a caring and respectful relationship.

6

CRAFTING SANCTUARIES - DIY PROJECTS FOR POLLINATOR ATTRACTIONS

"If the bee disappeared off the surface of the globe, then man would have only four years of life left. No more bees, no more pollination, no more plants, no more animals, no more man."

— *ALBERT EINSTEIN*

Have you ever wanted your garden to stand out, attracting not just neighbors but also bees, butterflies, and birds? Imagine your garden as a special retreat designed to offer the best experience for these visitors. In this chapter, we'll explore a few fun projects that will turn your garden into a favorite spot for pollinators, making them regular guests.

BUILDING BEE HOTELS: A HOME FOR SOLITARY BEES

Understanding Solitary Bees

Before you put up the "Vacancy" sign, you must understand who your guests are. North America is home to over 4,000 species of native bees. Only the **Honey Bees** build hives of beeswax comb. All other bee species are considered **Solitary Bees.** The solitary female bees build tube-shaped nests by themselves, using materials such as leaves, flower petals, bark, mud, and plants. Here, they lay their eggs in individual compartments. When the eggs develop, they chew their way out of the tunnel.

Bees forage close to their nests, so providing artificial nesting sites encourages nesting and pollination every year.

Design Principles

Bee hotels are the insect equivalent of a birdhouse, usually made of chunks of wood or bundled reeds. Unlike a birdhouse, though, bees do not crowd together in one room. They need individual cubby holes to crawl into.

Constructing a bee hotel involves more than just making holes in a block of wood. It's about knowing what different bee species need for a comfortable and safe place to nest. Here are some key ideas to consider:

- **Variety of hole sizes**: Different bee species like different hole sizes, from 2mm to 10mm. Having a variety of sizes attracts more types of bees.
- **Depth matters**: Holes should be 3-6 inches deep to allow enough space for multiple eggs and food storage.

- **Smooth interiors**: Rough edges can damage bees' delicate wings. To create a smooth surface, sand the edges down the holes.
- **Avoid treated wood**: Chemicals in treated wood can be harmful. Use only natural materials like untreated wood, bamboo, or reeds.

Materials and Construction

Bee Hotel

Of course, you can purchase bee hotels at nurseries, home improvement centers, and online. But, if you are crafty, you can build your own. Basic to elaborate instructions for building bee hotels are readily available online. Below is a basic plan, including tips for success:

Bamboo Cane Rooms

Materials Needed:

- 8' L x 8" W x 1" T of cedar or another durable wood source
- One box (approximately 25 screws) of 1-5/8" length coated or stainless steel
- Various 6" L x roughly 4" wide aspen/cottonwood (or other softwood) rounds
- An assortment of scrap woodcuts (2" x 4" or other)
- A ¼ " drill bit long enough to fully drill 6" through the above materials
- Reeds or bamboo canes. (You can purchase nesting reeds online if unavailable in your area.)

Instructions for Building a Bee Hotel:

- Cut two sides at 12" and bottom/top panels at 10".
- Pre-drill and fasten your box together.
- Cut two boards at 8-¾ " from the long edge of a 45-degree miter cut to the lower square edge.
- Join roof panels and use additional material to close off the backside of the house.

- Screw interior components and pack reeds into voids between components.
- Mount your bee house facing southeast to get morning sun. Make sure it is sheltered from wind and rain.

Tips:

- Use only natural, breathable materials such as wood, twigs, and plant stems, not plastic or glass.
- All tunnels should have smooth entrances free of splinters or cracks.
- Paper and cardboard tubes are OK to line drilled wooden tunnels, but not as stand-alone materials.
- Keep the total number of tunnels in a bee hotel under 100.
- In drilled blocks and grooved boards, nests should start at least 3/4" from the edge of the block or stack.

Placement and Maintenance

- _**First, a safety note**_**: It is crucial to keep bee hotels and nests away from your living areas to avoid bee stings and allergic reactions for you, your family, and your pets.**

Finding the perfect spot for your bee hotel is crucial for attracting bees. Consider these tips:

- **Sunny spots**: Place the hotel in a warm location that gets morning sunlight.
- **Protection from rain**: Position the hotel under an overhang to keep the nests dry.
- **Height**: To avoid predators like ants, the hotel should be at least three feet (one meter) off the ground.

154 | THE POLLINATOR GARDEN

- **Stability**: Securely attach or hang the bee hotel so it doesn't sway in the wind.

Making bee hotels helps our gardens flourish by providing bees with safe places to stay and making our local area more prosperous and vibrant.

CRAFTING BUTTERFLY PUDDLING STATIONS FOR SIPPING AND SUNNING

With their delicate wings and graceful flights, butterflies bring a magical touch to gardens. However, their survival depends on more than just nectar. They also need minerals and water for their health and reproduction. That's why having a puddling station is essential. It's like a spa retreat for butterflies, where they can drink water and get crucial minerals.

Butterfly Hydration Needs

Think of a butterfly's diet as a two-course meal. Nectar is the primary energy source, while minerals are crucial for their health and reproduction. Puddling stations act like fake little puddles that have essential minerals and salts. Male butterflies visit these spots to drink the mineral-filled water necessary for creating sperm. They then pass these minerals to the female during mating, ensuring healthier eggs. So, by installing a puddling station, you're not just giving butterflies a place to drink; you're supporting their life cycle.

DIY Puddling Station Designs

The beauty of a puddling station lies in its simplicity. You don't need elaborate materials or tools, just simple items found in nature. Here are some easy ideas:

- **Basic Sand and Salt Puddle**: Fill a shallow dish or a clay planter saucer with sand, mix in some potting soil or organic fertilizer, and sprinkle it with a pinch of table salt or rock salt. The sand/soil mixture should be somewhere between 1 and 2 inches. Add some small rocks or stones to serve as perches for the butterflies, ensuring the stones are higher than the level of sand. Keep the sand moist by adding water to create wet mud, and keep it moist. Butterflies will extract the water from the mud. Tip: Add slices of fruit to the dish.
- **Stone and Gravel Water Basin**: For a simple water basin, arrange smooth stone, gravel, or pebbles in a shallow bowl or saucer. Make sure some rocks stick out of the water so butterflies can land and drink safely without falling in.
- **Sponge Oasis**: Put a clean, wet, natural sponge on a plate for a safe drinking spot. The sponge's texture makes it easy for butterflies to land and drink. Adding a few stones to the plate should keep the plate from tipping over.

Butterflies on a dish of water and orange slices

Placement Tips

Choosing the right spot for your puddling station helps attract more butterflies and enhances the appearance of your garden. Here are some tips for picking the perfect place:

- **Sunshine is vital**: Place your puddling station in a sunny area. Butterflies are sun-loving creatures and are more likely to find the station if it's in a bright spot.
- **Protection from the wind**: Pick a place protected from the wind. This keeps the water from drying up fast and gives butterflies a peaceful place to drink and rest.
- **Visibility**: Set the station close to flowering plants in a clear, open area. This way, butterflies can easily find it while looking for nectar.

Maintenance Advice

Keeping your puddling station clean and appealing is simple but essential. Here's how to maintain it:

- **Refresh water regularly**: Evaporation and absorption can dry out your station. Add fresh water every day, making sure that there is no standing water to attract mosquitos.
- **Clean periodically**: Every few weeks, rinse the sand, stones, or sponge to stop mold and germs from growing, making the station a safe spot for butterflies.
- **Observe and adjust**: Notice how the butterflies use the station. If they don't visit often, move it to a place with more sun or change how much water you use.

With puddling stations, we're not just giving butterflies water. We're also providing them with vital minerals that help them reproduce successfully. This boosts the number and variety of butterflies in our gardens. By doing this simple thing, we improve our environment and ensure that future generations can enjoy the beautiful sight of butterflies.

BUILDING BIRDHOUSES, BATHS, AND FEEDERS - SUPPORTING OUR FEATHERED FRIENDS

Birdhouses are available at nurseries, home improvement centers, craft stores, and online. Alternatively, if you're handy, you can build one yourself. Remember, the structure should be tailored to the specific species you want to attract, as different birds prefer different sizes. For example, wrens need smaller houses, bluebirds need medium-sized ones, and robins require larger houses with an open front. Several websites and apps can help you identify local bird species, their nesting preferences, and the appropriate birdhouse dimensions.

For this subchapter, we will discuss instructions for a small, 4 x 5 1/2 inch birdhouse that will accommodate most small, single-dwelling birds. Below is a basic plan:

Building a Birdhouse

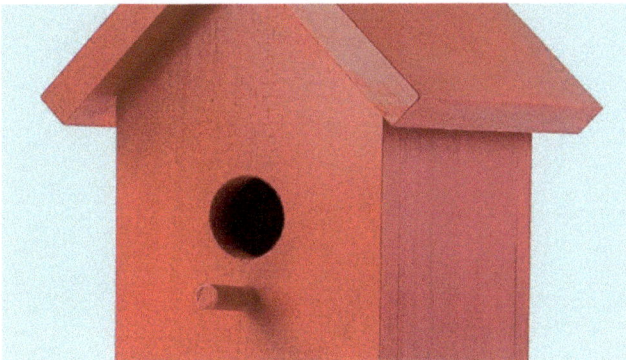

DIY Birdhouse

Tools

- Miter Saw
- Hand Saw With Miter Box (Optional)
- Power Sander
- Drill With Bits
- Clamps

Materials

- 1-in x 6-in x 6-ft Pine Board (Actual: 3/4-in x 5-1/2-in x 6-ft)
- 1/2-in Poplar Round Dowel
- Exterior Paint or Stain
- Wood Glue
- Painters Tape

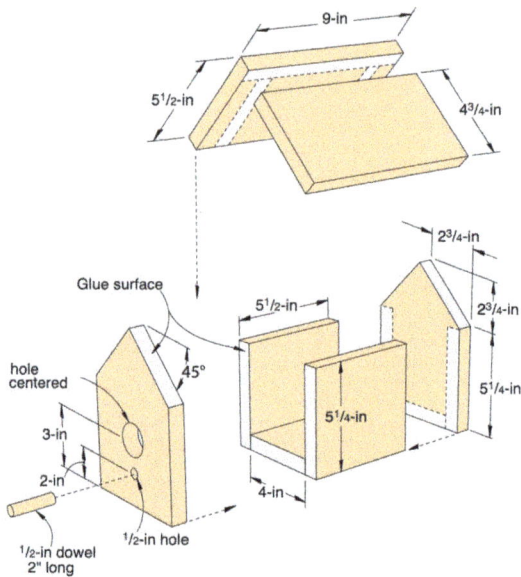

Basic Birdhouse Plans

- **Cut the Board and Perch**: Follow the Project and Cutting Diagram. Cut a 2-inch-long perch from a 1/2-inch dowel. Sand all the parts smooth with 150-grit sandpaper. Drill a 1-1/2-inch opening and a 1/2-inch hole for the perch on the front face. Sand the surfaces smooth and glue the perch in place. Glue and clamp the two sides to the back panel.
- **Assemble the Panels**: When the back and side joints are dry, glue and clamp the bottom and front.
- **Prepare the Roof**: Cut 3/4 inch off the length of one of the top panels. This will make the overhang even on both sides. Glue the roof panels together. Use painter's tape instead of a clamp.
- **Glue the Roof On**: Apply glue to the top edges of the front and back and set the roof assembly in place. Use painter's tape to secure the top while the glue dries.
- **Paint the House**: When the glue is dry, remove the tape and paint or stain the house. You can also drill a hook or screw to the roof to attach twine and hang it from a post or tree.

Birds enhance our gardens with their songs and colorful feathers and are crucial for pollination and spreading seeds. To attract them, we need to provide places for them to eat and bathe. This section will guide you through setting up bird baths and feeders that serve our feathered friends and add charm to our gardens.

Benefits of Bird Baths and Feeders

Bird Bath

Bird baths and feeders are more than just garden accessories; they're lifelines for birds, providing essential resources:

- **Nutritional support**: Feeders filled with seeds, nuts, and suet offer birds a reliable food source, especially when natural sources are hard to find, like winter or migration periods.
- **Hydration and hygiene**: Bird baths offer a place for birds to drink and bathe, necessary for their feather care and cooling off in hot weather.

Bird Feeder

- **Attracting diversity**: Different types of feeders and baths can attract a wide range of birds, from the smallest hummingbirds to the majestic hawks, each helping the garden in their own way.

Hummingbird Feeder

By including baths and feeders in your garden, you create a

welcoming environment for birds, encouraging them to visit and stay, which helps with natural pest control and pollination.

Design and Installation

Choosing and installing bird baths and feeders requires thoughtful consideration to ensure they are functional and safe for the birds and will look good in your garden:

- **Stability is vital**: Baths and feeders should be stable to avoid tipping. Bird baths need a rough surface for safe footing, and feeders should be durable in all weather.
- **Height matters**: Bird baths should be on the ground or slightly above to seem like natural water spots. Feeders should be placed at various heights by hanging them or using poles to attract different types of birds.
- **Shade and shelter**: For safety, locate them near bushes or trees. This placement allows birds to hide from predators quickly. However, keep enough distance to prevent ambushes by cats or other predators.

Setting up baths and feeders with safety and easy access in mind ensures a variety of birds will use and enjoy them.

Best Practices for Feeding

Feeding birds well involves understanding what they eat:

- **Varied diet**: Different birds have different dietary needs. Offer a variety of foods like seeds, fruits, nuts, and suet. For example, sunflower seeds attract many birds, while hummingbirds love nectar.

- **Quality matters**: Opt for fresh bird food to keep birds healthy and limit diseases.
- **Regular refills**: Keep feeders stocked, especially during peak feeding times such as migration periods and winter, to ensure a consistent food source for birds relying on them.

These practices help support a diverse and healthy bird community in your garden.

Water Safety and Maintenance

Keeping bird baths clean and safe is essential for the health of your garden visitors:

- **Freshness counts**: Replace the water every few days to stop algae and diseases. In warm weather, you should do this every day.
- **Cleaning routine**: Scrub bird baths often with a brush and mild bleach solution to kill harmful bacteria or viruses, and rinse them well so no bleach is left.
- **Winter care**: In freezing climates, use a heated bird bath or a heater to keep the water liquid so birds have water in winter.

Proper maintenance of bird baths makes them safe and welcoming, so birds will often visit your garden.

We welcome birds into our gardens by carefully choosing, setting up, and maintaining bird baths and feeders. These small steps make a big difference in supporting the health of local birds as pollinators and seed carriers. This turns our gardens into more than just beautiful sanctuaries for us; they are safe habitats for a variety of bird species.

DESIGNING FLOWER BOXES FOR BALCONIES AND SMALL SPACES

In cities with limited home gardening space, balconies and small patios can be essential spots for people and pollinators. We'll explain how to turn these small areas into attractive micro-gardens for pollinators with creatively designed flower boxes.

Maximizing Limited Spaces

The trick to using small spaces well is to think creatively, seeing them as places for vertical gardens, hanging pots, and layers of flower boxes. This gives you more room to garden and makes the space more appealing. Here's how to do it:

- **Vertical planting**: Use walls and railings to put up vertical planters or trellises, which will allow vines and climbing plants to grow higher, attracting pollinators.
- **Tiered flower boxes**: You can make or buy stacked boxes that go up vertically, allowing you to have many different plants in a small space.
- **Hanging baskets**: Hang baskets from ceilings or brackets and fill them with flowers that hang down to attract butterflies and bees.

Using vertical space, we transform areas thought too tiny for gardening into lively spots filled with plants frequented by pollinators.

Choosing the Right Plants

Selecting plants for your flower boxes is like planning a menu for a special meal and providing something for everyone. In city environments, where it's harder for pollinators to find food, selecting the right plants is crucial. Focus on these considerations:

- **Season-long bloomers**: Choose plants like petunias, marigolds, and zinnias that flower from spring to fall, giving pollinators a steady food source.
- **Native plants**: Select plants that are native to your area. They are well-suited to the local climate and pollinators, easier to care for, and offer more benefits.
- **Herbs and edibles**: Many herbs, such as basil, chives, and thyme, attract pollinators and are also helpful for cooking, making your garden both functional and supportive of pollinators.

In choosing these plants, we beautify our spaces and help support pollinators in the city.

DIY Flower Box Construction

Making your own flower boxes lets you add a personal style to your garden so you can tailor them to fit your space and style. Here's a simple guide to get started:

1. **Selecting materials**: Use untreated wood like cedar or redwood to avoid harmful chemicals. These woods are durable and resist rot.
2. **Designing for drainage**: Make sure your flower boxes have holes at the bottom for water to drain out, preventing root damage. A layer of gravel under the soil can help improve drainage.
3. **Sizing**: Customize your box sizes to fit your spot, such as a windowsill, patio, or balcony. Larger boxes hold moisture longer, which means less watering.
4. **Decoration**: Decorate your boxes with non-toxic paint or stains for a pop of color, or leave the wood bare for a natural, rustic look.

This project beautifies your outdoor space and offers a custom environment for pollinators, blending style with function.

Care and Maintenance

Caring for flower boxes in small spaces means paying close attention to their specific needs. Here are some tips to help your mini-gardens flourish:

- **Regular watering**: Flower boxes and containers lose water faster than soil on the ground, especially in sunny areas. Check how wet the soil is daily and water it to keep it slightly moist.
- **Feeding**: Feed your plants with a slow-release organic fertilizer for steady growth. Add liquid organic fertilizer for an extra boost during peak blooming periods.
- **Seasonal updates**: Swap out plants in your flower boxes to match the seasons: start with spring flowers, switch to summer blooms, and end with fall varieties to keep your display lively and welcoming to pollinators.

By following these tips, our small gardens stay vibrant and become safe havens for pollinators in the city. Each flower box proves that urban areas and nature can coexist beautifully, taking a small but meaningful move towards a world more welcoming to pollinators.

PLANTING A WILDFLOWER MEADOW IN ANY SIZE GARDEN

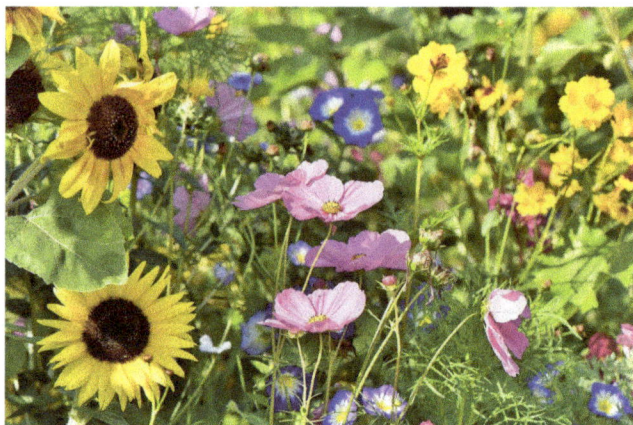

Wildflower Meadow

Imagine making even a tiny piece of land burst with colors and life. A wildflower meadow does just that, turning any garden spot or container into a lively, beautiful ecosystem that needs little care. This section will show you how to create your own wildflower haven that offers big benefits for both pollinators and people. Please also refer to *The Meadow Garden: Create a Low-Maintenance Wildflower and Native Plant Wonderland,* by author Dian Eaton, published in January, 2024.

Benefits of Wildflower Meadows

Wildflower meadows bring many environmental benefits, creating essential areas for pollinators by offering a wide range of nectar and pollen sources from different flowers. These meadows help many types of plants and animals thrive, attracting insects and birds. Aesthetically, wildflower meadows change throughout the year, showing off new colors and patterns with each season. This natural beauty offers a peaceful spot for people to enjoy and reflect.

Selecting Wildflower Species

For a great wildflower meadow, select plants native to your area. These plants have evolved with local pollinators and are used to your climate and soil conditions, making them resilient and easy to maintain. Here's how to start:

- Research native plant societies or local services for a list of area-specific wildflowers and seeds.
- Consider a mix of annuals for first-year color and perennials for lasting growth.
- Pick plants that flower at different times to give pollinators food all season.
- Choosing native plants helps your meadow support the local environment.

Preparation and Planting

Preparing the ground properly sets the stage for a thriving meadow. First, get rid of weeds and grass to lessen competition for sunlight and nutrients. You could use solarization or apply an organic herbicide carefully to keep the soil intact. After clearing the area:

- Check the soil to see what kind it is and adjust if needed. However, many wildflowers prefer soil that isn't too fertile.
- For small areas, scatter seeds with your hand. For big areas, use a seed spreader. Mixing the seeds with sand helps spread them more evenly.
- Use a rake lightly over the area so the seeds touch the soil but aren't buried too deep. This will prevent birds from eating the seeds.
- Water lightly to wet the soil and help seeds germinate. Keep the soil slightly damp until seedlings establish.

Be patient; perennials might take until the second year to flower, but annuals will add color earlier.

Ongoing Meadow Management

Once established, wildflower meadows don't need much care but do well with a little yearly maintenance to keep them healthy:

- **Annual mowing**: Once the flowers have stopped blooming and the seeds have spread, cut the meadow to manage any unwanted growth and prepare it up for the next season. Leave the trimmings out for a day to let seeds fall to the soil before clearing them away.

- **Selective weeding**: Look out for invasive plants that could overtake your wildflowers. Getting rid of them quickly can help prevent them from dominating.
- **Adding diversity**: With time, you may see some plants thrive and others fade. Bringing in new seeds or plants can help keep the balance.
- **Observation**: Regular walks through your meadow let you check on the health of your plants. It's also a perfect time to appreciate your efforts and spot visiting pollinators.

By taking these steps, you can create a beautiful wildflower meadow that not only helps local wildlife but gives pollinators a safe place in a world with fewer natural homes. With some planning, preparation, and patience, you can create a wildflower meadow that adds beauty and activity to your garden all year round.

SEED BOMBS: FUN AND EFFECTIVE WAYS TO SPREAD FLOWERS

Introduction to Seed Bombs

In the realm of gardening, few activities capture the imagination quite like the making and distribution of seed bombs (also known as seed balls). These small, potent packages are not just a way to introduce vibrant splashes of color to neglected or barren spaces; they're also a strategic tool in the guerrilla gardener's arsenal and a lifeline for pollinators seeking sustenance and shelter in urban jungles.

Seed Bombs

Making seed bombs is a simple and enjoyable activity for all ages that you can do at home. It's easy to find the materials, and the process allows you to enjoy some outdoor time, get your hands dirty, and learn about native plants. Seed bombs are fun for everyone, not just kids, and can even be a unique entertainment for social gatherings.

Seed bombs are the embodiment of hope and rebellion—a gesture that says, "Here, I plant life." They allow us to extend the reach of our gardens beyond the confines of our own spaces, supporting pollinators by creating pockets of wildflowers in unexpected places. Whether tossed into a forgotten corner of a community park or nestled into the crevices of urban decay, each seed bomb has the potential to burst forth with life, transforming spaces with the wild, untamed beauty of nature.

Crafting Seed Bombs with Native Wildflower Seeds

Creating seed bombs is a simple yet deeply satisfying process, one that invites us to get our hands dirty in the service of beauty and biodiversity. Here's how to create your own:

1. **Gather Your Materials**: You'll need clay powder (to bind the seeds and provide protection), compost (to offer nutrients), water, and native wildflower seeds (chosen for their adaptability to your local climate and their attractiveness to pollinators).

2. **Mix Your Ingredients**: Combine one part seeds, three parts compost, and five parts clay powder in a bowl. Gradually add water to the mixture until it has the consistency of playdough—it should hold together without crumbling but not be so wet that it sticks to your hands.

3. **Form the Bombs**: Pinch off small pieces of the mixture and roll them between your hands to form balls about the size of a marble. You want the ball small enough to dry quickly and break down easily. If you're making seed bombs with children, encourage them to shape the mixture any way they want. Seed "blobs" work too.

4. **Dry and Store**: Lay your seed bombs table covered with newspaper, or on a cookie sheet covered in aluminum foil. Let dry for 24-48 hours in a cool, dry place. Once hardened, they're ready to be deployed (thrown or scattered), or stored in a paper bag until you're ready to use them.

Best Practices for Scattering Seed Bombs

While the act of tossing a seed ball can feel delightfully chaotic, a few guidelines can help ensure that your efforts lead to germination and growth:

- **Timing is Everything**: Spring and autumn are ideal times for distributing seed bombs, aligning with the natural germination cycles of most wildflowers.

- **Location, Location, Location**: Choose spots of bare ground that receive plenty of sunlight and have some exposure to rain. While seed bombs are designed to thrive in tough conditions, giving them a fighting chance increases the likelihood of success. You want the seeds to directly contact the ground so that once rain hits them, they will break down. Then you wait for the flowers to bloom. And they will.
- **Respect the Environment**: Only use seed bombs in areas where they're unlikely to disrupt existing ecosystems, and never introduce non-native species to wild areas.

Engaging the Community

Seed bomb-making is more than a gardening activity; it's a powerful way to connect with others and spread awareness about the importance of native plants and pollinators:

- **Workshops**: Host a seed bomb-making workshop at local schools, libraries, or community centers. It's a fantastic way to educate people of all ages about the role of pollinators and the importance of native plants.
- **Community Events**: Coordinate with local environmental groups to organize seed bomb toss events in areas that could benefit from a floral facelift.
- **Gifts**: Package your seed bombs in attractive, eco-friendly materials and give them as gifts to friends, family, and neighbors. Include information on why they're essential for pollinators and how to distribute them.

Through these activities, seed bombs become a catalyst for community engagement, education, and action. They offer a hands-on way for people to contribute to the health of their local ecosystems, one wildflower at a time.

PERENNIAL SHRUBS AND TREES THAT PROVIDE YEAR-ROUND BENEFITS

Every garden has the potential to become a special sanctuary that makes us happy and helps local pollinators. The secret is adding perennial shrubs and trees. These structural plants are the backbone of garden design and are vital for giving pollinators food and shelter throughout the year.

Importance of Structural Plants

Perennial shrubs and trees play a big role in helping pollinators. They add beauty and privacy and also give important resources to pollinators. In colder months, when there are fewer food sources, these plants continue to offer food with their berries or late blooms. Their branches and leaves also provide shelter for pollinators from predators and the weather, making them essential for a healthy pollinator-friendly garden.

Selecting the Right Species

Choosing the right shrubs and trees can seem daunting, but focusing on a few key characteristics can simplify the process:

- **Native varieties**: Look for plants that are native to your region. These plants have co-evolved with local pollinators and are more likely to provide the resources they need.
- **Bloom time**: Choose plants with different blooming times so your garden has something for pollinators all year.

Early blooming flowers feed emerging pollinators, and late blooming flowers provide food sources before winter.

- **Evergreens**: Consider adding evergreen shrubs and trees. They not only keep your garden colorful in winter but also provide year-round shelter for pollinators.

When selecting these plants, consider the types of pollinators you want to attract. Some plant species may be particularly beneficial for butterflies, while others might cater more to bees or birds.

Incorporating into Garden Design

Integrating these structural plants into your garden design can add both function and form:

- **Layering**: Position taller trees as a backdrop, with shorter shrubs in front. This creates a pleasing, layered look that resembles natural habitats.
- **Clusters**: Group trees and shrubs together. This forms shelters and keeps pollinators in one area, making pollination more effective.
- **Feature plants**: Choose striking trees or shrubs as highlights in your garden. A beautifully flowering dogwood or a berry-laden holly can draw the eye as well as pollinators.

Through thoughtful placement and selection, these plants can enhance the beauty of your garden while helping the environment.

Maintenance and Care

Taking care of your perennial shrubs and trees to help support pollinators includes a few key steps:

- **Pruning**: Prune regularly to help maintain the health and shape of your plants. Just make sure to do it at the right time, as some plants need last year's growth to bloom.
- **Watering**: Water newly planted shrubs and trees regularly until they're established. Even afterwards, during dry spells, supplemental watering can help prevent stress.
- **Mulching**: Apply a layer of mulch around your plants to help maintain moisture, stop weed growth, and improve the soil quality as it breaks down.

Adding perennial shrubs and trees to our gardens does more than beautify our spaces. We create a refuge that provides food and shelter for pollinators year-round. This helps the environment around us and makes us feel closer to nature, showing how important our role is in supporting biodiversity.

Finishing our look at DIY projects to attract pollinators, it's clear every action, like planting wildflowers, making a bee hotel, butterfly puddler, bird baths, birdhouse, seed bombs, or choosing the right plants, contributes to a larger purpose. We're not just gardening; we're stewarding the earth, one pollinator-friendly project at a time.

7

ENGAGING WITH THE COMMUNITY: BECOMING A POLLINATOR ADVOCATE

> *"Never doubt that a small group of thoughtful, committed citizens can change the world; indeed, it's the only thing that ever has."*
>
> — *MARGARET MEAD*

SPEAK UP: YOU HAVE SOMETHING TO SAY

Once your pollinator-friendly garden is thriving, expect visits from curious neighbors, family, and friends. They'll likely want to visit your garden and learn how to create one of their own. Show them around. Answer their questions. Explain how important it is to get interested in pollinators: who they are, how they work, what they need, and why we need them.

Put a Sign on It

Install a sign in your yard to announce that you have a Pollinator-Friendly Garden. This can draw attention and spark conversations within the gardening community. Pollinator signs are available at home improvement stores, nurseries, and online platforms like Etsy and Amazon. Be proud. Celebrate your garden!

Take the Next Step

To further engage with your interests, consider joining garden clubs, schools, or community organizations to share your experiences. You might also join an environmental or civic organization to help plan community-wide pollinator-friendly gardens. At the very least, you will always have a subject you can discuss with ease, knowledge, and pride.

Take pride in your achievements. Your dedication and success have established you as a Pollinator Advocate.

CONCLUSION

> "Once we start to act, hope is everywhere. So instead of looking for hope, look for action. Then, and only then, hope will come."
>
> — *GRETA THUNBURG*

We've been on an incredible journey through *The Pollinator Garden*, witnessing the complex relationships between plants and animals working together for the benefit of all. For instance, we've learned how bees and butterflies assist plant reproduction through pollination; in return, those plants nourish the pollinators. We learned that certain animals spread seeds, aiding plant growth in new areas, and in response, plants offer shelter to many animals. This intricate balance of nature forms the foundation for the survival of all living beings. We've become aware of the threats vital pollinators face and armed ourselves with the knowledge and tools to help them, starting in our own gardens.

We met the unsung heroes of our ecosystems: the pollinators, including bees, butterflies, birds, and many more, who play a critical role in our food supply and the health of our planet. We learned how much we rely on these tiny pollinators and how to give back to them. This includes choosing the right native plants from our regions that provide food for pollinators and adopting sustainable gardening practices that keep our gardens thriving without harming the very creatures we aim to support.

We delved into simple do-it-yourself projects such as bee hotels, butterfly puddlers, birdhouses, and various inventive methods to make our areas more attractive and provide secure havens for pollinators.

I encourage you, no matter how big or small your space, to take a step, plant a seed, and watch as life blossoms around you. Speak up for pollinators, fight for their safety, and teach others how easy it is to help these vital members of our ecosystems. As a pollinator-friendly gardener, you are now an advocate. You hold the power. Let's make every flower count, every garden a sanctuary, and every action a step towards a healthier, more vibrant planet.

Happy gardening!

Dian Eaton

BIRDS, BEES, AND BUTTERFLIES, PLEASE!

Your Chance to Lead Others Down the Garden Path

By sharing your honest opinion of THE POLLINATOR GARDEN, you'll help fellow gardeners find the information they're searching for to "pay it forward" and create a thriving, native plant, pollinator-friendly garden.

Thank you so much for your support. Your review will have more impact than you might imagine.

Scan the QR code below to leave your review!

ABOUT THE AUTHOR

Dian Eaton is an author of gardening books, young adult, and children's books. *The Pollinator Garden: How to Attract Nature's Heroes - Planting for Birds, Bees, and Butterflies* is the second in a series of sustainable gardening books. The first book, *The Meadow Garden: Create a Low-Maintenance Wildflower and Native Plant Wonderland,* was published in January 2024. Dian is also a painter, actor, and songwriter. She has a degree in Theater Arts and has performed on stage, in films, and on television. Dian lives with her family in Southern California and pursues her passions: gardening, writing, and painting.

RESOURCES

For more information on pollinators, conservation programs, and wildlife organizations, here are some wonderful sites to visit:

- American Horticultural Society www.ahsgardening.org
- Xerces Society (for all things pollinators) at www.xerces.org
- Pollinator Conservation Program https://www.xerces.org/pollinator-conservation
- The Bee Conservancy https://thebeeconservancy.org/
- Lady Bird Wildflower Center www.wildflower.org
- National Invasive Species Information Center www.invasivespeciesinfo.gov/subject/identification
- National Wildlife Federation https://www.nwf.org/
- San Diego Zoo Wildlife Alliance www.sdzwa.org
- USDA U.S. Department of Agriculture https://www.usda.gov/
- U.S. Fish and Wildlife Service https://www.fws.gov/
- US Forest Service www.fs.usda.gov/managing-land/wildflowers/pollinators/importance

REFERENCES

- Attenborough, David quotes https://www.goodreads.com/quotes/search/david+attenborough
- Einstein, Albert quotes https://lwww.goodreads.com/search/quotes/albert+einstein
- Hawken, Paul quotes https://www.goodreads.com/search/quotes/paul+hawken
- Hyde Bailey, Liberty https://www.brainyquote.com/authors/liberty-hyde-bailey-quotes
- Jefferson, Thomas quotes https://goodreads.com/search/quotes/thomas+jefferson
- Mead, Margaret quotes https://goodreads.com/search/quotes/margaret+mead
- Page, Russell quotes https://www.goodreads.com/search/quotes/russell+page
- Thunburg, Greta quotes https://www.brainyquote.com/authors/greta+thunburg
- *Why is Pollination Important? | US Forest Service* https://www.fs.usda.gov/managing-land/wildflowers/pollinators/importance
- *How to Create a Bee-Friendly Landscape* https://extension.umaine.edu/gardening/manual/ecology/how-to-create-a-bee-friendly-landscape/#:
- *Evaluating the Impact of Commonly Used Pesticides ...* https://www.ncbi.nlm.nih.gov/pmc/articles/PMC10081893/
- *Creating Urban Pollinator Hot Spots | Pollinator.org* https://www.pollinator.org/creating-urban-pollinator-hot-spots
- *Pollinator-Friendly Native Plant Lists* https://xerces.org/pollinator-conservation/pollinator-friendly-plant-lists
- *DIY a Water Feature for Pollinators* https://savethebee.org/diy-a-water-feature-for-bees-and-pollinators-a-step-by-step-guide/
- *How to build a bee hotel* https://www.woodlandtrust.org.uk/blog/2020/04/how-to-build-a-bee-hotel/
- *Native Plants and Ecosystem Services* https://www.canr.msu.edu/nativeplants/ecosystem_services
- *Native Plants for Pollinators and Beneficial Insects* https://xerces.org/

publications/plant-lists/native-plants-for-pollinators-and-beneficial-insects-northeast

- *Identification | National Invasive Species Information Center* https://www.invasivespeciesinfo.gov/subject/identification
- *How to build a pollinator garden* https://www.fws.gov/story/how-build-pollinator-garden
- *Pollinator Health* https://www.organic-center.org/pollinator-health
- *5 Homemade Pesticides: DIY Soap Sprays for Plants* https://www.almanac.com/organic-pesticides#:
- *How to Make Compost in 4 Easy Steps* https://www.thespruce.com/how-to-make-compost-p2-1761841
- *Harvesting Rainwater for Use in the Garden* https://extension.oregonstate.edu/catalog/pub/em-9101-harvesting-rainwater-use-garden
- *How to Build a Hotel for Wild Bees - Treehugger* https://www.treehugger.com/how-build-hotel-wild-bees-4863814
- *DIY Butterfly Puddler - Garden Gate Magazine* https://www.gardengatemagazine.com/articles/diy-projects/wildlife-pollinator/diy-butterfly-puddler/#:
- *Attract Birds With Birdbaths* https://www.allaboutbirds.org/news/attract-birds-with-birdbaths/
- *Seeds and Plants for Pollinators* https://www.pollinator.org/shop/seeds
- *How to build a pollinator garden* https://www.fws.gov/story/how-build-pollinator-garden
- *PollinateTO Grants - City of Toronto* https://www.toronto.ca/services-payments/water-environment/environmental-grants-incentives/pollinateto-community-grants/
- *Pollinator Conservation Program* https://www.xerces.org/pollinator-conservation

PHOTO REFERENCES

- Emily Thopson. Goldenrod [Image]. Unsplash https://unsplash.com/photos/goldenrod
- Laura Ockel. Witch Hazel [Image]. Unsplash https://unsplash.com/photos/witch-hazel
- Pexels - Honey Bee - 460961 Honey Bee
- Pexels - skitterphoto - 3780 Bumble Bee
- Pexels - lyn - ryan - 18057792 Hummingbird
- Pexels - jeffry - surianto - 11553324 Sunbird
- Pexels - erik - karits - 9344812 Flowerpecker

- Pexels - part-of-life - 1558922 Honeyeater
- Pexels - colin - dobson - 1893218 Bananaquit
- Pexels - tonia - krankman - 1160879 Bellbird
- Pexels - jean - paul - montanaro - 15549020 Honeycreeper
- Pexels - egor - kamelev - 149661 Butterfly
- Pexels - skyler - ewing - 13132850 Monarch Butterflies
- Pexels - alen - kuzmanovic - 3433 Moth
- Pexels - egor - kamelev - 1114318 Beetle
- Pixabay - bat - 1713607 _ 1280 Bat
- Pexels - nikolett - emmert - 14608860 Ladybug
- Vecteezy - diagram - pollination - of - flowering - plants _ 615
- USFWS - rusty - patched - bumble - bee - medium Rusty-Patched Bumble Bee
- Pexels - chait - gole - 2892245 Monarch Butterfly
- Pixabay - nature - 3242718 _ 1280 crocus in snow Crocus
- Pixabay - spring - 1166564 _ 1280 snowdrops Snowdrops
- Pixabay - lavenders - 1595584 _ 1280 Lavender
- Pixabay - bee-balm - 1043110 _ 1280 Bee Balm
- Pexels - yusule - furugya - 10004390 Goldenrod
- Pixabay - new - england - asters - 6603427 _ 1280 New England Aster
- Pixabay - conversation - 3513843-1280 - Birds in Bowl
- Pixabay - joe-pye-weed - 380026 Joe-Pye Weed
- Pixabay - mountain - mint - 4574003 _ 1280 Mountain Mint
- Pexels - tom - fisk - 18071995 Wild Columbine
- Pexels - jeffrey - riley - 7501037 Spring Beauty
- Pixabay - witch - hazel - 2655742 _ 1280 Witch Hazel
- Pexels - hanna - tomany - 804805 Swamp Milkweed
- Pexels - chris - f - 8382126 Southern Magnolia
- Pexels - petr - ganaj - 4096492 Purple Cornflower
- Pexels - manuel - torres - garcia - 199347 Bottlebrush Buckeye
- Pexels - joris - eschalier - 192495 Cherokee Rose
- Pixabay - flowers - 7397663 _ 1280 Prairie Blazing Star
- Pexels - elena - golovchenko - 8182543 Wild Geranium
- Pexels - jeffrey - surianto - 17920956 Red Columbine
- Pexels - rohan - deuangan - 2844320 - 10723566 Switchgrass
- Pexels - guang - I - udo - 15532733 Milkweed
- Pexels - yesmeurys - matco - 18784378 Sunflower
- Pixabay - indian - paintbrush - 5708664_1280 Indian (Seaside) Paintbrush
- Pixabay - pensteman - 3678049 _ 1280 Rocky mountain Penstemon

- Pixels - tom - fisk - 13087944 Colorado Blue Columbine
- Pexels - Karen - irala - 14425533 Desert Marigold
- Pexels - kindel - media - 8979692 Joshua Tree
- Pixabay - california - poppy - 1362728 _ 1280 California Poppy
- Pixabay - common - 87460 _ 1280 Soap Plant
- Pixabay - succulents - 3693409 _ 1280 Succulents
- Pixabay - sagebrush - 2360542 _ 1280 Sagebrush
- Pexels - ekaterina - belinskaya - 4921883 Agave
- Pexels - yufan - jiang - 19897151 Yucca
- Pixabay - cholla - cactus - 458076 _ 1280 Cholla Cactus Flower
- Pexels - petr - ganaj - 4105714 Prickly Pear Cactus
- Pexels - phillippe - serraud - 18860041 Mesquite Tree
- Pixabay - purple - loosestrife - common - 5259367 _ 1280 Purple Loosestrife
- Pixabay - English - ivy - 1255 English Ivy
- Pexels - nikolett - emmert - 14608860 Ladybug
- Pexels - nadi-lindsay - 17814646 Lacewing
- Pexels - phil - mitchell - 18779897 Hoverfly
- Pexels - cajko - 139896 - 423604 Dandelion
- Gettyimages - 845116606 - 200 Clover Flower
- Pixabay - lavenders - 1595584 _ 1280 Lavender
- Pexels - nikiemmert - 20596135 Sedum
- Pixabay - sage - leaves - plant - full - width Sage
- Pixabay - ornamental - grass - 455209_1208 Ornamental Grass
- Pixabay - insect - hotel - 883096 _ 1280 Bee Hotel
- Pexels - umsiedlungen - 16532211 Bee Hotel Cane Rooms
- Pixabay - brown - sailor - 784970_1280 Brown Sailor Butterfly
- Pixabay - red - birdhouse - 101929658 Birdhouse
- Pixabay - birdhouse - project - design- plans Birdhouse Plans
- Pexels - david - levinson - 1390763 Bird Bath
- Pexels - chris - f - 13604285 Hummingbird feeder
- Pexels - damir - 12301873 Window Flower Box
- Pixabay - flowers - 3598555 _ 1280 Wildflower Garden
- Pixabay - seed - bombs - 2314498 _ 1280 Seed Bombs

www.ingramcontent.com/pod-product-compliance
Lightning Source LLC
Chambersburg PA
CBHW041930260326
41914CB00009B/1246